Mark A. Noll

PROTESTANTISM

A Very Short Introduction

OXFORD

UNIVERSITY PRESS

OXFORD

UNIVERSITY PRESS

Great Clarendon Street, Oxford OX2 6DP

Oxford University Press is a department of the University of Oxford.
It furthers the University's objective of excellence in research, scholarship,
and education by publishing worldwide in

Oxford New York

Auckland Cape Town Dar es Salaam Hong Kong Karachi
Kuala Lumpur Madrid Melbourne Mexico City Nairobi
New Delhi Shanghai Taipei Toronto

With offices in

Argentina Austria Brazil Chile Czech Republic France Greece
Guatemala Hungary Italy Japan Poland Portugal Singapore
South Korea Switzerland Thailand Turkey Ukraine Vietnam

Oxford is a registered trade mark of Oxford University Press
in the UK and in certain other countries

Published in the United States
by Oxford University Press Inc., New York

British Library Cataloguing in Publication Data

Data available

Library of Congress Cataloging in Publication Data

Data available

Typeset by SPI Publisher Services, Pondicherry, India
Printed in Great Britain by
Ashford Colour Press Ltd, Gosport, Hampshire

ISBN: 978–0–19–956097–4

1 3 5 7 9 10 8 6 4 2

To Joel Carpenter

POSTSTRUCTURALISM Catherine Belsey
PREHISTORY Chris Gosden
PRESOCRATIC PHILOSOPHY
    Catherine Osborne
PRIVACY Raymond Wacks
PROGRESSIVISM Walter Nugent
PROTESTANTISM Mark A. Noll
PSYCHIATRY Tom Burns
PSYCHOLOGY
    Gillian Butler and Freda McManus
PURITANISM Francis J. Bremer
THE QUAKERS Pink Dandelion
QUANTUM THEORY
    John Polkinghorne
RACISM Ali Rattansi
THE REAGAN REVOLUTION Gil Troy
THE REFORMATION Peter Marshall
RELATIVITY Russell Stannard
RELIGION IN AMERICA Timothy Beal
THE RENAISSANCE Jerry Brotton
RENAISSANCE ART
    Geraldine A. Johnson
RISK Baruch Fischhoff and John Kadvany
ROMAN BRITAIN Peter Salway
THE ROMAN EMPIRE Christopher Kelly
ROMANTICISM Michael Ferber
ROUSSEAU Robert Wokler
RUSSELL A. C. Grayling
RUSSIAN LITERATURE Catriona Kelly
THE RUSSIAN REVOLUTION
    S. A. Smith
SCHIZOPHRENIA
    Chris Frith and Eve Johnstone
SCHOPENHAUER Christopher Janaway
SCIENCE AND RELIGION Thomas Dixon
SCIENCE FICTION David Seed
THE SCIENTIFIC REVOLUTION
    Lawrence M. Principe
SCOTLAND Rab Houston

SEXUALITY Véronique Mottier
SHAKESPEARE Germaine Greer
SIKHISM Eleanor Nesbitt
SOCIAL AND CULTURAL
    ANTHROPOLOGY
    John Monaghan and Peter Just
SOCIALISM Michael Newman
SOCIOLOGY Steve Bruce
SOCRATES C. C. W. Taylor
THE SOVIET UNION Stephen Lovell
THE SPANISH CIVIL WAR
    Helen Graham
SPANISH LITERATURE Jo Labanyi
SPINOZA Roger Scruton
STATISTICS David J. Hand
STUART BRITAIN John Morrill
SUPERCONDUCTIVITY
    Stephen Blundell
TERRORISM Charles Townshend
THEOLOGY David F. Ford
THOMAS AQUINAS Fergus Kerr
TOCQUEVILLE Harvey C. Mansfield
TRAGEDY Adrian Poole
THE TUDORS John Guy
TWENTIETH-CENTURY BRITAIN
    Kenneth O. Morgan
THE UNITED NATIONS
    Jussi M. Hanhimäki
THE U.S. CONGRESS Donald A. Ritchie
UTOPIANISM Lyman Tower Sargent
THE VIKINGS Julian Richards
VIRUSES Dorothy H. Crawford
WITCHCRAFT Malcolm Gaskill
WITTGENSTEIN A. C. Grayling
WORLD MUSIC Philip Bohlman
THE WORLD TRADE
    ORGANIZATION Amrita Narlikar
WRITING AND SCRIPT
    Andrew Robinson

Available soon:

DICTIONARIES Lynda Mugglestone
DEVELOPMENTAL BIOLOGY
    Lewis Wolpert

DERRIDA Simon Glendinning
MADNESS Andrew Scull
MULTICULTURALISM Ali Rattansi

For more information visit our website
www.oup.com/vsi/

Contents

Acknowledgements

I am especially grateful to those who have instructed me in the wider worlds of Protestant history whether in person, through mind-altering books, or by example. Chief among those teachers have been Daniel Bays, Stephen Kang, David Martin, Martin Marty, Dana Robert, Lamin Sanneh, Andrew Walls, and David Wells. For this particular book, I owe a special debt to authors whose unpublished works I have put to use, including Ann Cashner (African Lutherans), Raully Donahue (League of Nations), Kara Fromke (the Scudder family), Nicholas Miller (American religious freedom and Seventh-Day Adventists), Mary Venables (Duke Ernst the Pious), and Genzo Yamamoto (Nitobe Inazo). A few of the paragraphs are adapted from my book *Turning Points: Decisive Moments in the History of Christianity*, 2nd edn. (Baker Books, 2001). As always, Maggie Noll has been indispensable. The book is dedicated to a friend and comrade-in-arms who has also been more of an instructor than he realizes.

List of illustrations

Protestantism

Introduction

Protestants today are all over the map, literally and figuratively. Recent commemorations underscore this global presence. In Germany, the 500th anniversary of Martin Luther's birth in 1983 generated conferences, books, and widely noted celebrations for the German monk who sparked the Reformation that led to Protestantism as a distinct form of Western Christianity. The same took place in Switzerland in 2009 when numerous public events marked the 500th anniversary of the birth of John Calvin, who, from his post in Geneva, had defined a theological agenda for almost all Protestants and shaped what became the Presbyterian and Reformed denominations. And so it had gone in 1985, also in Germany, to mark the 300th anniversary of Johann Sebastian Bach, the Kapellmeister and composer who has been the most significant Protestant contributor to musical history; and in 2003 in America when scholars and active church people mounted celebrations for the 300th birthday of Jonathan Edwards, the last of the great Puritan theologians and the first of the great American revivalists.

This last round of anniversaries, however, differed significantly from what had taken place in previous centuries. This time Martin Luther was celebrated by large Lutheran communions in Tanzania and Madagascar, as well as in northern Europe and the United States. Calvin events took place in Argentina and Ghana as well as in Switzerland and the United States. Bach was remembered in Japan and Romania as well as in Germany, while commemorations for Edwards were held in South Korea and South Africa as well as in America.

Extraordinary diversity

Contemporary Protestant diversity is much more than just geographical. Church traditions that trace their origins to the earliest days of the European Reformation – including Lutherans, Presbyterians, Anglicans, Mennonites, and several Reformed denominations – or that arose in Europe and America during the 17th and 18th centuries (Congregationalists as well as many varieties of Methodists and Baptists) are now found throughout the world. But for Protestantism outside of Europe and North America, Pentecostal and local independent churches, which are a product of only the last century, have come to play a much larger role. Even in Europe, while the traditional churches retain considerable influence, the most active congregations are often Pentecostal, sometimes filled with newcomers from Africa or the Caribbean. Amazingly, one of Europe's largest churches today is the Embassy of the Blessed Kingdom of God for All Nations in Kiev, which was founded only in 1994 by Sunday Adelaja, a Nigerian Pentecostal who had come to study in the Soviet Union before the collapse of communism.

Modern forms of Protestantism are even stronger outside of Europe. For some years, the world's largest local congregation of any kind has been the Yoido Full Gospel Church in Seoul, Korea. It was founded as recently as 1958 by a young Pentecostal, David Yonggi Cho, and his mother-in-law, Ja-shil Choi, both pastors of the Assemblies of God, a denomination linked to the largest of the United States' white Pentecostal churches. The church's website in 2010 tallied its membership at over 763,000, or more than in many Western denominations of long standing.

1. The Yoido Full Gospel Church in Seoul, Korea, has for some years been the largest Protestant congregation in the world

The Pentecostal fixation on Scripture continues a central commitment of historic Protestantism, while Pentecostal ideals for Christian life extend themes first popularized by John Wesley, a founder of Methodism. Yet Pentecostalism began as a protest against religious formalism in already existing churches, including Protestant churches. Moreover, the ardent Pentecostal focus on the New Testament's Book of Acts, especially the miraculous gifts of the Holy Spirit that are described there, has weakened ties to historic Protestant traditions, even as it has driven a great expansion of Protestantism worldwide.

The Yoido Full Gospel Church in Seoul illustrates both continuities and discontinuities with the Protestant past. It is organized along small-group principles and so imitates reforming European Protestants of the late 17th century. Pastor Cho's ministry also features many standard elements of evangelical Protestant teaching. But his stress on the immediate apprehension of God's direct presence, on the possibility of miraculous physical

3

healing, and on the promise of economic wellbeing for those who exercise faith make him more representative of Protestantism in the wider world today than of what had been traditional in Europe and North America.

Many other signs point to the multiform character of contemporary Protestantism. In the United States – the nation with the largest number of adherents to Protestant or Protestant-like churches – the denominations descended directly from the Reformation, or at one remove, sustain intense internal debates over whether and how to modify their religious inheritance. Some of the flashpoints concern Christian doctrine (like the character of Holy Scripture), others address questions of Christian practice (like the proper attitude toward homosexuality), and still others problems of social engagement (like the type and degree of political involvement). The result is genuine difficulty in defining *the* Protestant position on any theological or social issue.

Moreover, significant movements within contemporary Protestantism show scant concern for what were once defining Protestant characteristics. The American megachurch phenomenon provides a striking illustration. Megachurches are defined as congregations with an average weekly attendance of 2,000 or more. As of 2010, researchers counted about 1,400 of such congregations unevenly distributed in the United States – 195 in California and 191 in Texas, but only 8 in Massachusetts. A few of the megachurches are identifiably Lutheran, Presbyterian, or Methodist. Many more are Baptist. But the clear majority, including the largest, with weekly attendance reaching 20,000 and even higher, are Pentecostal, non-denominational, or independent. Their style of worship features music keyed to contemporary popular taste rather than drawn from historical Protestant hymnody; their appeal is geared to contemporary consumer culture; their consciousness of the past is thin.

Some coherence nonetheless

Despite rampant Protestant pluralism, it is still possible to identify general beliefs and practices that have marked most Protestants in most places at most times. Historically considered, Protestantism is an all-inclusive term for religious movements descended directly or indirectly from the 16th-century Reformation in which Martin Luther and John Calvin played leading roles. Through the 19th century, the great majority of Protestants, despite ever-present internal conflicts, were self-conscious about that heritage and also strongly united in their opposition to Catholicism. Increasingly over the last century, however, it makes more and more sense to define 'Protestantism' as Christian movements, not Catholic or Eastern Orthodox, that are marked by a characteristic message, a characteristic standard of authority, characteristic forms of organization, and characteristic styles of activity. The message proclaims salvation as a gift from God that brings reconciliation with God and among people on earth. The authority is the Christian Bible. The forms of organization tend to the local and the participatory. The activities feature individual activity and responsibility.

Traditionally, the Protestant message of salvation has taken for granted that humans are sinners who have offended God, the holy and perfect creator, by focusing selfishly on their own self-interests. It specifies that God himself provides the remedy for sin in the perfect life, sacrificial death, and miraculous resurrection of Jesus Christ, the second person of the Trinity. It goes on to teach that new spiritual life in Christ is made active by the Holy Spirit who renews ordinary believers, guides church communions in God-honouring worship, and encourages believers in self-sacrificing service to fellow humans.

An immense range of variations has existed among Protestants in fleshing out this general picture of salvation. European and American Protestants have debated each other endlessly concerning the relative weight of divine initiative and human responsibility in the process. More recent controversy has swirled over how to understand the miraculous elements in this story of salvation. The last issue has not troubled most of the world's newer Protestant movements, though they are engaged in intense debate over issues like the nature of spiritual combat between the Holy Spirit and the devil, or how salvation in Christ may come to ancestors who died before the Christian message arrived.

The earliest Protestants agreed that the message of salvation was taught authoritatively in the Christian Scriptures which, they held, had been obscured by the corruptions of Roman Catholicism. In 1638, the Englishman William Chillingworth published a polemical work aimed at Roman Catholics in which he boldly proclaimed, 'the BIBLE, I say, the BIBLE only, is the religion of Protestants'. Chillingworth, as a supporter of King Charles I, also happened to be engaged in polemics against the Puritans, who shortly thereafter took up arms against the king, over how best to understand the Scriptures that both Chillingworth and the Puritans embraced. Yet the many internal disputes of that sort should not be allowed to obscure the authoritative importance of the Bible for all Protestants. That common allegiance, in fact, is probably the best reason why it is still possible to speak, in admittedly very general terms, about a common Protestant history.

In the contemporary world, the impact of Scripture has been multiplied many times over by the efforts of Bible translators, most of them Protestant, who have undertaken Herculean labours in rendering the Scriptures into non-Western languages. It is a sign of new Protestant realities that one of the largest Bible publishers today is the Amity Foundation, established in 1987 by the United Bible Societies and the China Christian Council, which as of 2010 had published over 60 million copies of the Scriptures in various Chinese dialects and other languages as well.

2. The Amity Printing Company in China is now one of the world's major publishers of Bibles

Protestant loyalty to a principle defined in the Reformation era as 'the priesthood of all believers' explains much about Protestant organization and activity. Many Protestants possess some form of church hierarchy, as bishops or superintendents with Anglicans, Lutherans, Moravians, and some Pentecostals; regional synods with Presbyterians and the Reformed; or local and national conferences with Methodists. But populist, entrepreneurial, and democratic forces have always tempered, and sometimes overwhelmed, unifying Protestant organization. The early stress by Luther, Calvin, and other founders on 'vocation' as applied to every believer – and to the believers' responsibilities in the world as well as to religious duties – spurred a strong predisposition to vigorous activism.

A religious movement that began by protesting the Catholic church has been marked by the renewing (and fragmenting) protests of many other reformers, the creative (and disputatious) energy of self-selected leaders, and the committed (and ever expanding) efforts of dedicated lay women and men. The ramifications of 'the priesthood of all believers' strongly distinguished the early centuries of Protestant history in Europe and North America. They have become even more pronounced recently in the extraordinary proliferation of Protestant movements throughout the world.

Through the centuries, observers have also seen a number of affinities between Protestant religious practice and broader cultural influence. Frequent claims that Protestantism supports a liberal, or even democratic, political order and that Protestantism enjoys a mutually supporting relationship with capitalism have generated much careful scholarship and much sloppy punditry. Links between Protestantism and modern science have also been debated, with the general consensus that at least some Protestants stimulated the rise of early modern science while in more recent periods other Protestants have contested the results of modern scientific practice. With the recent decline of traditional Christianity in Europe and the explosion of Protestant-like faith elsewhere, a few discerning historians have been asking about connections between Protestantism and secularization. Questions include whether the Protestant attack on Roman Catholic authority led eventually to an assault on all Christian authority, but also whether the individual adaptability characteristic of Protestant faith has made it well suited to the disruptions caused by commercial and cultural globalization.

Statistical overview

World Protestant adherents

	1910	2010
Europe	58%	12%
United States	31%	15%
Rest of the world	11%	73%

It is challenging to write a coherent history because of the sheer multiplicity of Protestant and Protestant-like churches in the world today. The *Atlas of World Christianity*, published in 2010, counts more than 4,000,000 individual congregations worldwide, with most of them gathered into more than 38,000 Protestant denominations.

Information from this atlas also outlines a geographical history. Until the early 1800s, nearly all Protestants lived in the European regions where Protestantism had emerged nearly three centuries earlier. After the passage of another century, in 1910, of the world's approximately 157 million adherents to Protestant and Protestant-type churches, almost three-fifths still were in Europe. (The four European countries with the largest Protestant populations – Germany, Britain, Sweden, and the Netherlands – accounted for nearly half the world total.) Yet also by 1910, the United States had become the world's leading Protestant nation, with nearly a third (31%) of world adherents.

Changes in world Protestantism from 1910 to 2010 have been breathtaking. By 2010, of the world's approximately 875 million Protestant or Protestant-type adherents, less than 12% lived in Europe. Another 15% lived in the United States. In former European colonies like South Africa and New Zealand, the numbers of Protestants have burgeoned, but mostly in non-white churches. By the 21st century, Protestantism had become a primarily non-Western religion. In 1910, 79% of the world's Anglicans lived in Britain (with most of the rest in the United States and the British commonwealth). By contrast, in 2010, 59% of the world's Anglicans were found in Africa. Also in 2010, more Protestants lived in India than in Germany or Britain. About as many lived in Brazil as in Germany and Britain combined. Almost as many lived in each of Nigeria and China as in all of Europe. Much more than ever before, the Protestant world has become co-extensive with the world itself.

(For some of the specialized terms used in this introduction, there is a glossary at the end of the book.)

Chapter 1
Reformation beginnings

The Reformation that gave birth to Protestantism began with a local protest in a small German town on 31 October 1517. Martin Luther, a 34-year-old monk of the Augustinian order, had earnestly been seeking peace with God by practising the rigours of his monastic calling. As he put it many years later, 'Though I lived as a monk without reproach, I felt that I was a sinner before God with an extremely disturbed conscience. I could not believe that he was placated by my satisfaction' – that is, by Luther's own efforts to do what God required. Luther's protest of October 1517 charged the Catholic church with, in effect, failing to help in his hour of need. He was looking to the church for wisdom, comfort, and reassurance, but he perceived an institution preoccupied with earthly power, wealth, and influence.

In 1517, Luther was troubled specifically about indulgences, the officially authorized certificates that individuals could purchase to lessen the time that deceased relatives or friends spent in purgatory. Johannes Tetzel, a particularly aggressive salesman, had been busy near Luther's small city of Wittenberg in Saxony. Luther was incensed. He and (as would soon become evident) many others were looking to the church for deep spiritual counsel, but the church seemed to be offering only a superficial fire sale. It was customary for university professors like Luther to address controversial questions by proposing theses for debate. Thus, he drew up ninety-five of such theses where the surface issue was trivialization of the indulgence system, but where the underlying question was the meaning of Christianity itself.

To Luther, the crass selling of forgiveness represented much that had gone wrong with the church. Through his intensive study of Scripture he was coming to a set of firm convictions: forgiveness was God's gift, not a human prerogative; it stemmed from divine grace, not from something that people did for themselves; it meant a change of heart, not a business transaction; it was freely given because of Christ's sacrificial death on the cross, not sold to the gullible by a huckster. And so Luther offered his Ninety Five Theses for debate. The story is fairly reliable that he nailed them to the door of his town's castle church.

Europe in transition

When enterprising printers translated Luther's original Latin document into German and marketed it aggressively, he became an immediate cause célèbre. Much of the controversy came from the specifically religious issues under debate. But it also involved a great deal more than religion narrowly understood.

In politics, Protestants would have made little headway if there had not already existed local rulers and urban councils eager to assert their prerogatives over against the far-away authority of Pope and Emperor. Economic changes also strengthened local centres of influence, even as they undercut deference to traditional authorities. With trade, population, and agricultural production on the upswing, money became a growing point of friction between the church and local rulers. As trade and circulating money increased, the power of land-based nobles weakened, while the influence of city-based merchants, lawyers, and master craftsmen increased. These groups did not yet constitute a modern 'middle class', but the seeds were being planted for the growth of self-sustaining civil society. At the bottom of the social ladder, peasants were exchanging feudal obligations for contractual and money duties. In short, all levels of society were being forced to renegotiate their once settled connections.

Intellectual life had also entered a new day. Johann Gutenberg's printing press, perfected in the 1450s, greatly accelerated the transformation. Not the least of its influences was stimulation for reading and publishing that Protestant movements would exploit in spreading throughout Europe. Closer to 1500, printed books sped the circulation of new intellectual fashions that historians call the Renaissance. Efforts by Francisco Ximénez de Cisneros of Spain and Desiderius Erasmus of Rotterdam, older contemporaries of Martin Luther, to publish a purified text of the New Testament in its original Greek bespoke the general desire to refresh European life through a return to classical sources. Earnest searching for authentic ancient texts – Latin and Greek, pagan and Christian – had been an ongoing European preoccupation for several generations before Protestants deployed the authority of one of those ancient texts, the Bible, to challenge magisterial Catholic teaching.

The Church in crisis

As important as broader European developments were for Protestant beginnings, conditions in the Catholic church constituted the primary cause. Since early in the 14th century, Western Christianity had reeled from crisis to crisis. First was the 'captivity' of the papacy by French monarchs who beginning in 1309 moved the seat of Roman Catholicism to Avignon near the southern border of France. Then came the Great Schism, 1378 to 1415, when competing claimants for the papal tiara divided Europe into rival camps. Protestants would later remember that the Council of Constance (1414–18), which succeeded in uniting Europe around a single pope, revealed its lack of concern for broader reform by how it treated Jan Hus. Hus was a Czech reformer who spoke out against church corruption, preached in the vernacular, and championed the Bible as the norm for Christian living. For these efforts, and in a tangle of contested political alliances, the Council of Constance in 1415 burned him at the stake.

Reforming councils helped considerably in restoring order to the church's external life, even as its spiritual life was strengthened with new devotional works like *The Imitation of Christ* by Thomas à Kempis. But the leadership of the church was adrift. The era's 'Renaissance popes' were conspicuous for military power, gaudy displays of wealth, and sometimes gross immoralities, but not for spiritual dedication.

The pope who had to deal with Luther's Ninety Five Theses was Leo X (1513–21) who showed more concern for promoting church teachings and cleaning up corruption than his immediate predecessors. But his passion for new buildings and for the arts also drove him to orgies of profligate spending. It was in fact an indulgence authorized by Leo X to fund the building of St Peter's basilica in Rome that Tetzel was selling in the neighbourhood of Wittenberg.

Yet abuse and corruption were not the most basic problem. Luther was joined by a growing number who were most troubled that the church at its highest levels was not tending to the most fundamental questions: What does God require of humans? Why do humans fall short of God's requirements? What can bridge the gap between a holy God and people painfully aware of their own sinfulness?

Many within late-medieval Catholicism – like Ximénez, Erasmus, or Ignatius Loyola who founded the Jesuits – pursued reform within the church. Protestants felt they had to abandon Catholicism in order to find what they desperately required.

Luther's life outlines the Protestant future

A burst of publishing energy in a single year, 1520, allowed Luther to stake out positions that became foundational for Protestantism as a whole. First, his *Treatise of Good Works* defined faith in Christ as humanity's only truly good deed and as itself a gift of God's grace. Then his *Papacy at Rome* argued that, if the pope, or any other church officer, did not help people find God's free grace in Christ, they should be considered 'Anti-Christ'. An *Address to the Christian Nobility of the German Nation* urged Germany's rulers to stop ceding control of their political and economic, as well as spiritual, lives to the pope. *The Freedom of the Christian* tried to show how liberation in Christ led on to good works. In a characteristically paradoxical phrase, Luther wrote: 'A Christian is a perfectly free lord of all, subject to none. A Christian is a perfectly dutiful servant of all, subject to all.'

The title of Luther's most important book in that year of extraordinary publication evoked the papacy's earlier tenure in Avignon, but this time applied to the spiritual realm: *The Babylonian Captivity of the Church*. This polemic described official church teaching on the sacraments as a system of bondage. The only true sacraments – baptism, the Lord's Supper, and perhaps confession – were those that Christ had himself instituted and that joined the promise of grace with a physical sign. They were never to be hemmed in with man-made regulations or put up for sale to the highest bidder. Luther held that the rest of the church's seven sacraments (confirmation, marriage, holy orders, extreme unction) had become tools to entangle, entrap, and encumber the faithful.

Luther on justification by faith

One of the many places where Luther spelled out his convictions about justification by faith alone was in *The Babylonian Captivity of the Church* from 1520:

If the mass is a promise . . . , then access to it is to be gained, not with any works, or powers, or merits of one's own, but by

> faith alone. For where there is the Word of the promising God, there must necessarily be the faith of the accepting man. It is plain therefore, that the beginning of our salvation is a faith which clings to the Word of the promising God, who, without any effort on our part, in free and unmerited mercy takes the initiative and offer us the word of his promise.... In no other way can man come to God or deal with him through faith. that is to say, that the author of salvation is not man, by any works of his own, but God, through his promise; and that all things depend on, and are upheld and preserved by, the word of his power, through which he brought us forth, to be a kind of first fruits of his creatures.

Luther's great fusillade was too much. In response, Pope Leo X issued a bull, *Exsurge Domine*, that pleaded with God to arise and rebuke this 'wild boar from the forest' of Germany. Then the young Habsburg Holy Roman Emperor, Charles V, demanded that Luther appear before an imperial Diet scheduled in central Germany for the spring of 1521 to show why he should not be declared an outlaw and, presumably, suffer the same fate as Jan Hus. The Diet was to convene at Worms, a small city on the Rhine that became synonymous with the beginning of Protestantism.

At Worms, Luther was shown a table full of his writings and asked to recant. After saying he would gladly take back a few incautious words, Luther addressed a resolute defence to the emperor and the imperial court:

> Since then your serene majesty and your lordships seek a simple answer, I will give it...: Unless I am convinced by the testimony of the Scriptures or by clear reason (for I do not trust either in the pope or in councils alone, since it is well known that they have often erred and contradicted themselves), I am bound by the Scriptures I have quoted and my conscience is captive to the Word of God.

> I cannot and I will not retract anything, since it is neither safe nor right to go against conscience.

Luther may then have added, 'Here I stand. I can do no other. God help me. Amen.'

Commentators beyond number have scrutinized the significance of these words. Protestants usually emphasize Luther's appeal to Scripture as the final norm for guiding Christian life and correcting Christian institutions. Catholics – as well as historians of Western liberty, individualism, and secularization – have emphasized Luther's appeal to his own conscience. The day after Luther made his famous speech, Charles V questioned the ability of any individual to stand over against the testimony of tradition: 'It is certain that a single friar errs in his opinion which is against all of Christendom and according to which all of Christianity will be and will always have been in error both in the past thousand years and even more in the present.' Whether the emperor was right or wrong, he had shrewdly perceived that when the appeal to conscience joined the appeal to Scripture, something new had arrived in Western Christian history.

Five weeks after Luther's appearance at the Diet, Charles V issued the edict that made Luther an outlaw. But by that time, Luther's prince, Frederick, Elector of Saxony – known to Protestants as 'Frederick the Wise' – had spirited the maverick monk into hiding at Wartburg Castle, an isolated Saxon fortress near Eisleben where Johann Sebastian Bach would later be born. In his isolation, Luther worked furiously at translating the New Testament into German. Using the Greek text as published by Erasmus, instead of the Latin Vulgate that was the Catholics' official Bible, Luther finished this task in less than three months. The full New Testament was published in 1522, with many revisions and editions to follow until Luther's death in 1546. The translation of the Bible into the common language so that all could read it for themselves was firmly fixed as a foundation of Protestantism.

What Luther found in the Bible has also had a great impact on later history, even if the commitment to Scripture has always prevailed more widely than the specific teachings he drew from the Bible. The centre of Luther's theology was the cross of Christ. He held that everything in Christianity hinges on understanding how and why Christ, the Son of God, suffered and died for sinners. To be a Christian was personally to enter into Christ's death by suffering the destruction of the self's claim to stand before God. Only in being united with Christ's death could the believer then experience the renewing power of his resurrection.

Although Luther's teaching often sounded radical, his own efforts at preparing materials for worship and daily Christian instruction were conservative. When in 1526 he published the *German Mass*, it retained much of the traditional Catholic prayers and worship order, which continues to guide Lutherans around the world to this day. It was even more consequential for illustrating a general matter: Protestant worship practices are for the most part locally determined and continually negotiated, rather than being uniform and directed by central church authorities.

Just as important as formal liturgies was Luther's effort to supply fresh devotional and teaching material. In 1529, Luther himself prepared a *Small Catechism* that offered (and continues to offer) a succinct, mostly non-polemical, and Christ-centred form of instruction. But far and away Luther's most important stimulus to ordinary religious life was his promotion of hymn-singing. Almost as soon as he returned from the Wartburg to resume his duties in Wittenberg, he began preparing hymns to sing in gathered worship and in the home. Some hymns he had sung as a monk. More were fairly wooden versifications of the Apostles' Creed, the Lord's Prayer, and the Ten Commandments. Others, like a loose paraphrase of Psalm 130 published in 1523 or the famous Christianization of Psalm 46 that came a few years later ('A Mighty Fortress Is Our God'), provided powerful poetical meditations on his main theological convictions.

Luther's paraphrase of Psalm 130

From trouble deep I cry to thee
Lord God hear thou my crying;

...

Although our sin be great, God's grace
Is greater to relieve us;
His hand in helping nothing stays,
The hurt however grievous.
The Shepherd good alone is he,
Who will at last set Israel free,
From all and every trespass.

Protestants would later differ among themselves, often passionately, over whether hymns should stick close to paraphrasing Scripture or address more general Christian themes. The type of music used with hymns – or even whether any music should be used at all – soon became contested points that still distinguish Protestants from each other. But for teaching, consoling, challenging, encouraging, and uniting, hymnody in its various forms became the lifeblood of Protestantism from the start.

Luther's significance for later Protestant history was extended by his marriage in 1525 to Katharina von Bora, a former nun who had left the convent when Luther attacked traditional Catholic vows as a form of salvation by works. Originally his purpose in marrying was to show foes that he opposed monasticism in practice as well as in theory. But eventually he came to enjoy a warm and loving relationship with Katharina, to heed at least some of her counsels in restraining his head-strong behaviour, and to deeply cherish the six children born to their union. For Protestantism as a whole, Luther's example exalted the status of wives, mothers, and the domestic round. His successful marriage contributed greatly to establishing a general Protestant conviction: the belief that any calling – whether in the home or in public, sacred or secular, taken up by men or by women – could be pursued honourably and for the glory of God.

Spreading and diversifying

The term 'Protestant' emerged in 1529 from a political confrontation. At another imperial Diet, this one held at Speyer in the Rhineland, one of the princes who had embraced Luther's teaching, Landgraf Philipp of Hesse, successfully organized the German leaders who shared his convictions. Their 'protest' against Charles V's efforts to restore the religious unity of the Empire emphasized what had already become a standard Protestant appeal:

> We are determined by God's grace and aid to abide by God's Word alone, the holy gospel contained in the biblical books of the Old and New Testaments. This Word alone should be preached, and nothing that is contrary to it.

The reference to 'the holy gospel' highlighted another term that in those early years enjoyed a broader currency than 'Protestant'. From the Greek word for 'gospel', *euangelion*, the reformers and their supporters were known as 'evangelicals'.

Soon, however, it became obvious that Protestantism was much more than just Martin Luther writ large. Within just a few more years at least four more 'protests' against traditional Roman Catholicism had emerged.

First in time was a reform movement in Zurich led by Ulrich Zwingli, a Catholic priest well trained in the new Renaissance scholarship. Zwingli's life course strikingly paralleled Luther's, including influence from Erasmus' Greek edition of the New Testament, protests against abuses in the indulgence trade, and popular preaching from the New Testament that electrified Zurich citizens. At a public disputation in 1523 Zwingli laid out his objections against Catholic errors in the Mass, the Catholic prohibition against clerical marriage, and the subordination of civic rulers to religious authorities in matters belonging to the state. He then defined his highest allegiance: 'I offer to defend and vindicate [these views] with Scripture…. I am ready to be corrected, but only from the same Scripture.'

Zwingli's arguments convinced the Zurich town fathers to renounce their Catholic bishop and to establish a reformed church order that went further than Luther's had gone. For example, although Zwingli himself was an accomplished musician, the Zurich reform banished musical instruments from church because Zwingli could find no explicit warrant in Scripture for their use in public worship.

Shortly before his death in 1529, when he was killed on the field of battle while supporting Zurich against its Catholic opponents, Zwingli also took part in an event that showed how difficult it would be to erect a single reformed church. Philipp of Hesse, who had united the 'Protestant' princes of the Holy Roman Empire to stand against Charles V, wanted to carry that work of unity further. Yet he knew that Luther in Wittenberg and Zwingli in Zurich interpreted the Lord's Supper (or Eucharist) differently. Philipp, hoping to achieve the same united front among the theologians as he had achieved with the rulers, called them to the city of Marburg in Hesse, one team led by Luther and another by Zwingli.

At their meeting, the theologians agreed on what reform should mean for almost all points of doctrine and practice – except when it came to the Lord's Supper. For Luther, Christ was truly present in the elements of bread and wine, through which God acted graciously to truly communicate the benefits of Christ's saving death. For Zwingli, Christ's presence in the elements was symbolic; thus, the value of the rite was the stimulus it gave believers to thank God for their redemption. From a modern perspective, it might not seem as if this was an insuperable difference. But in a context where the Catholic mass had been the focus of faith, doctrine, church authority, and personal hope, evangelical differences over how to reform the mass became supremely significant.

Inability to resolve this crucial difference set a permanent course for Protestantism. The reforms that Luther, Zwingli, and many others were advocating led to Protestant *churches* rather than a single reform of the one Western church. Protestant disunity would never be as bad as Catholics, as well as some Protestants, have charged. Common allegiance to Scripture and a general agreement on most elements in the historic creeds made it possible for many Protestants to cooperate fairly well with each other. Yet the fissure that was manifest at Marburg in 1529 anticipated the divisions that remain a prominent feature of Protestantism to this day.

The Anabaptists

The next Protestant variety was a spin-off from the reform in Zurich. It occurred when several of Zwingli's most active followers urged him to go further with his reforming efforts. The leaders of these 'Swiss brethren' included Conrad Grebel, the son of a merchant who had been drawn into the Zurich circle by Zwingli's powerful preaching, and George Blaurock, a priest who followed Zwingli's lead in forsaking the priesthood and taking a wife.

These zealous young men wholeheartedly agreed with Zwingli that the Bible should be the only source of religious authority, but they interpreted Scripture more radically. In their reading, they found no justification for civil support of the church, they rejected participation in warfare, and they denied that the state had a right to punish heretics. Zurich's radical reformers became known as 'Anabaptists' (or 're-baptizers') because they rejected the baptism of infants and insisted that individuals should be baptized only after making a personal profession of faith.

These Anabaptists represented the opening wedge of 'radical reform' that pushed biblical interpretations into uncharted waters. They were especially reviled for rejecting the long-established connections between church and state. And so retribution was swift and violent. Felix Manz, once an ardent disciple of Zwingli, became the first Anabaptist martyr when he was executed by his fellow Zurich Protestants on 5 January 1527. The mode of execution – drowning in Lake Zurich – was chosen to mock his stance on baptism. Michael Sattler, a former Benedictine monk, was executed soon thereafter, but not before he helped author the Schleitheim Confession that spelled out clearly where the Anabaptists differed from the main Protestant reformers.

The Schleitheim Confession

From the Anabaptist's Schleitheim Confession (1527):

> Dear brethren and sisters, we who have been assembled in the Lord at Schleitheim on the Border, make known...that as concerns us we are of one mind to abide in the Lord as God's obedient children, [His] sons and daughters, we who have been and shall be separated from the world in everything, [and] completely at peace....

> First. Observe concerning baptism: Baptism shall be given to all those who have learned repentance and amendment of life, and who believe truly that their sins are taken away by Christ.... This excludes all infant baptism, the highest and chief abomination of the pope....

> Sixth. We are agreed as follows concerning the sword:
> The sword is ordained of God outside the perfection of
> Christ. . . . . In the perfection of Christ, however, only the ban
> is used for a warning and for the excommunication of the one
> who has sinned, without putting the flesh to death, - simply
> the warning and the command to sin no more.

The Anabaptist movement was stabilized by the work of Menno
Simons, a Dutch Catholic priest who converted to Protestantism
in the mid-1530s. Simons, from whom contemporary Mennonites
trace their origin, was particularly important for making
Christian pacifism a foundational principle, which clearly
differentiated the Anabaptists from some of the era's other radical
reformers who were willing to use violence in pursuit of a
reformed Kingdom of God.

The Anabaptists were a tiny minority in the 16th century, despised
by both Protestants and Catholics for seeming to threaten
Christian civilization itself. But their break with the enmeshed
church-state ties of traditional European Christendom was
exceedingly important. While only a very few later Protestants
have followed the Anabaptists to embrace pacifism, the
Anabaptist stance on religious freedom would become the
standard for Protestants throughout the world and for most
Catholics and Orthodox as well.

John Calvin and reform in Geneva

More influential than the Zurich or Anabaptist reforms was the
reformation that took place in Geneva, Switzerland. The key
figure here was John Calvin, a French-educated legal scholar who
had ended up in Geneva when Catholic resistance stiffened
against Protestant efforts in France. In 1536, the Geneva city

councils opted for reform; shortly thereafter the fiery preacher, William Farel, who had been instrumental in pushing Geneva toward Protestantism, constrained Calvin to take his place as the city's religious mentor. Farel recognized Calvin's unusual ability that was on display in his 1536 book, the *Institutes of the Christian Religion*, a work that would later expand through many editions, alternating French and Latin, to become the most impressive early statement of Protestant theology. The more than 1,000 pages of this work rested upon many more thousand pages of biblical sermons and biblical lectures that Calvin produced regularly throughout his entire adult life. Especially memorable in these commentaries was Calvin's development of the biblical theme of covenant, which joined God's choice of Old Testament Israel with the merciful revelation of Christ in the New Testament ('testament' is another word for 'covenant') – and all under the rubric of merciful divine promises. Especially memorable in the *Institutes* was Calvin's picture of Christ as the perfect prophet, all-sufficient priest, and merciful king. Calvin also taught that God's decisive action was foundational for the salvation of human beings. This was his famous doctrine of predestination whereby God, for the manifestation of his own glory, before the foundation of the world and without respect to human merits, decreed who would be saved (and, by implication, damned). Yet Calvin's account of predestination differed hardly at all from what Luther had offered; only later would predestination become the key doctrine identified with Calvin's legacy.

Calvin's reforming rather than radical approach took several years to take hold in Geneva. Repeated clashes with the city's leaders centred on who would control religious teaching and guide the new reforms. Calvin's insistence on the supremacy of church leaders in these spheres earned him a two-year exile at one stage, but eventually he prevailed and was able to implement what he considered a properly biblical pattern of reform. One key was Presbyterian organization which drew leading laymen alongside Geneva's ministers in guiding the church. This church order, along with his comprehensive approach to reforming all aspects of Geneva's moral and social life (schools, hospitals, poor relief, even the taverns), soon made Geneva a model for others who wanted to follow biblical principles in reconstructing Christian civilization on Protestant principles.

The shape of reform that Calvin largely succeeded in bringing to Geneva became an inspiration for many others in Europe and eventually even in New England. Although 'Calvinism' was in many ways only an extension of 'Lutheranism', by showing how the Protestant desire of having Scripture reform every aspect of life could be carried out practically and with discipline, Calvin's influence eventually came to exceed that of the German reformer.

The English Reformation

The era's final reform with great continuing influence took place in England. While the other main Protestant movements involved cooperation between leaders of church and state, in England, government clearly led, with religion following along behind.

The desire of England's monarch, Henry VIII, to secure a legitimate male heir to his throne was the immediate cause for reforming the English church. Because Henry's original wife, Catherine of Aragon, had produced only one child, a female (who would later reign as Queen Mary from 1553 to 1558), he entered into negotiations with the pope for permission to divorce Catherine and marry again. Catherine, however, was an aunt of Charles V, which made the pope, who needed the Emperor's protection, unwilling to allow a divorce. In 1532, events came to a head when Anne Boleyn, Henry's prospective new wife, became pregnant. In order to ensure that the child would be legitimate, Henry got the leader of the Church in England to issue a decree annulling his union with Catherine and allowing a marriage to the pregnant Anne.

That leader was Thomas Cranmer, a cautious bureaucrat and loyal servant of the crown, but also a scholar with strong, though well-hidden, leanings toward the new reforms. With the willing help of Henry's chief advisor, Thomas Cromwell, Cranmer had in fact been working behind the scenes to advance Protestant measures. Others in England were ready, including a network of Cambridge scholars who had been reading Luther's works, the remnants of an earlier populist movement (the Lollards) that had circulated copies of Scripture in English, and the dedicated scholar William Tyndale whose lifelong passion was to provide a fresh, up-to-date translation of the Bible. Soon after his divorce and new marriage, Henry, with Cranmer and Cromwell assisting, secured a formal declaration from Parliament – 'that the King our Sovereign Lord, his heirs and successors, kings of this realm, shall be taken, accepted, and reputed the only Supreme Head on earth of the Church of England, called *Anglicana Ecclesia* (the Anglican Church)'.

Once Henry had broken with the pope, it was still not clear what the character of *Anglicana Ecclesia* would be. His chief goal was to preserve his own independence. As a result, when loyal Catholics like the Lord Chancellor, Sir Thomas More, refused to disavow their allegiance to Rome, Henry reacted ruthlessly by sending More to the block.

Yet Henry was by no means enamoured with Martin Luther. As a young man, he had won from the pope a coveted title, *Fidei*

THE booke of the common prayer and administration of the Sacramentes, and other rites and ceremonies of the Churche: after the vse of the Churche of Englande.

LONDINI, in officina Richardi Graftoni, Regij impressoris.

Cum priuilegio ad imprimendum solum.

Anno Domini. M.D.XLIX. Mense Martij.

3. The *Book of Common Prayer* that Thomas Cranmer compiled in 1549 set the Anglican Church on a moderate course of Protestant reform

Defensor (defender of the faith, a title still carried by British monarchs), when he published a rejoinder under his name to Luther's *Babylonian Captivity of the Church*. Even after the rupture with Rome, Henry ordered several English clerics who had become outspoken proponents of Luther's teaching burned at the stake.

Still, because of Henry's marriage to Anne Boleyn space did open up for Cranmer, with Cromwell's assistance, to promote distribution of the Scriptures in English, appoint reform-minded bishops, and bide his time for a further opportunity. That opportunity arrived when Henry's only legitimate son (by his third wife, Jane Seymour) succeeded to the throne in 1547. During the short reign of Edward VI, Cranmer and his allies in 1549 published a new guide for public worship, the *Book of Common Prayer*. They also completed work on a statement of Christian belief, the Forty Two Articles, but only just in time to be issued in 1553 shortly before the death of the young king. All Protestant reforms were then rolled back under Edwards' Catholic half-sister, Mary. But during the reign of Elizabeth (1558–1603), the daughter of Anne Boleyn and the third of Henry's children to ascend the throne, a moderate Protestant stance was secured for the realm. Elizabeth issued a revised *Book of Common Prayer* and abridged the doctrinal statement of Edward's reign into Thirty Nine Articles that were closer to Calvin's teachings than to Luther's. In her attention to religion, however, Elizabeth primarily shared her father's main concern to develop a stable church under tight state control.

Throughout much of its history, Anglicanism has included a self-consciously Catholic element that minimizes the 16th-century break from Rome. But that element has never been more than a minority. Moreover, when in the later centuries Britain became the world's most extensive imperial power, the Anglicanism that accompanied the empire to the colonies usually pushed in a self-consciously Protestant direction.

Chapter 2
Protestant Christendom

From the early 16th century well into the 18th, most Protestants saw themselves carrying out the reform of European Christendom. Although self-consciously opposed to Roman Catholicism, most Protestants joined Catholics in taking for granted the norms of 'Christendom'. As ably defined by historian Hugh McLeod, Christendom describes:

> a society where there are close ties between leaders of the church and secular elites; where the laws purport to be based on Christian principles; where, apart from certain clearly defined outsider communities, everyone is assumed to be Christian; and where Christianity provides a common language, shared alike by the devout and the religiously lukewarm.

With such an all-encompassing vision, and with Europe now divided religiously, conflict was inevitable.

A last-ditch effort to mediate Catholic–Protestant differences did take place at a colloquy held in Bavaria at Regensburg in 1541. But despite an unexpected agreement on the hotly contested question of justification by faith, the Protestant and Catholic negotiators could not agree on how to define a properly authoritative church. The Catholics' Council of Trent, which convened episodically from 1545 to 1563, hardened Catholic positions on the era's controversial religious questions. A series of learned Protestant responses to Trent, including one by Calvin, cemented the European divide into hostile religious camps. In 1555, through the Peace of Augsburg, which ended a war between the Emperor and German Lutheran princes, Lutheran principalities won the right to institute Lutheranism as the official religion of their territories. Reformed or Calvinist regions soon were granted the same right in practice, although not fully recognized until the mid-17th century. With the enthronement of Queen Elizabeth in 1563, England also moved decisively into the Protestant roster of nations.

A confessional era

Historians of early-modern Germany have coined the term 'confessionalization' to describe Europe from the mid-16th to the early 18th century. They are describing a competitive system of political, religious, and cultural organization that combined tight management of local government with uniform religious practice. One church for one area remained the norm, but now with Protestant alternatives. Except for a few radical Protestants, opposition to Roman Catholicism did not mean support for religious freedom in a modern sense.

Confessions

The 'confessional age' was given this name by the era's major statements of Christian faith:

The Augsburg Confession (1530) for Lutherans in Germany (in Sweden, the Latin Augustana);

The First and Second Helvetic Confessions (1536, 1562) for the Reformed in Switzerland;

The Thirty Nine Articles (revised 1571) for England;

The Canons and Decrees of the Council of Trent (1545–63) for Catholic regimes;

The Heidelberg Catechism (1563) for the Reformed in Germany and the Netherlands;

The Book of Concord (1580) for German Lutherans;

The Scots Confession (1560), and then the Westminster Confession (1646) for Scotland.

Lutherans took the lead in organizing their own principalities, electorates, and cities. But soon after Luther's death, intramural theological strife and the defeat of Lutheran troops by the armies of the Emperor pushed Lutheranism back into Prussia, Saxony, other German lands, and the Scandinavian kingdoms. In these regions, Lutheranism remained a powerful force – in fact, to this day. But Lutheranism was also mostly bottled up until in later centuries emigrants and missionaries took Lutheranism, but not Lutheran Christendom, overseas.

By contrast, Reformed or Calvinist Protestantism continued to expand as a religious and social force throughout the early modern era. Calvin's Geneva became the cockpit for a Reformed Internationale because of its hospitality to refugees from Catholic countries. It remained a lodestar because Geneva's doctrinal teaching, its effective social control, and its experiments in institution building were particularly attractive to others who sought root and branch reform. Reformed theology was similar to Lutheran theology in many ways. One of the differences, however, had long-lasting effects. Followers of Luther expanded several of his insights to create a theory of 'two kingdoms' that postulated one set of principles for the church and another for the civil sphere. A tendency toward social quietism was the result. It was otherwise in France, much of Switzerland, the Netherlands, south-western

Germany, Hungary, Scotland, and with some factions in England where Reformed theology pushed decidedly toward activism.

Compared to Lutheran confessionalism, Reformed regimes were more dynamic in pursuing distinctly Protestant programmes of political theory and practice, philosophy, science, and art. The Reformed gave more responsibility and initiative to the laity. They also had a much greater capacity for generating disagreement among themselves.

France, the Netherlands, and Scotland

In France, Reformed convictions inspired the Huguenots who came close to winning control of the nation toward the end of the 16th century before they were overwhelmed by resurgent Catholic power.

The story in the Netherlands was similar inasmuch as strong Reformed convictions undergirded a long struggle to throw over the Catholic rule of Habsburg Spain. Dutch Reformed history came to differ from French Reformed history, however, when the Protestants won. Almost as soon as independence was secured, Holland's Protestant theologians took off after each other in protracted controversy over how best to understand God's provision of human salvation. The result was a synod convened in 1618 at Dort by leaders of the Dutch Republic. This synod repudiated the teachings of Jacob Arminius, who had defined a larger role for human agency in choosing or rejecting the gospel. It affirmed five theological principles that are often presented as a simple epitome of 'Calvinism', even though Calvin never put his own theology together in just this way. (The five points, which yielded the acronym TULIP were Total human depravity, God's Unconditional election of the redeemed, atonement Limited to only those who would be redeemed, God's Irresistible grace for those who would be redeemed, and the Perseverance of the elect.)

In perhaps an ironic reaction to the intensity of these debates, Dutch authorities edged toward a policy of religious toleration that anticipated modern ideals of religious freedom.

Compared to the Netherlands, Scotland established an even more comprehensive Reformed nation. The early leader was John Knox, a bold preacher who had spent two years as a French galley slave for his reformation preaching in the 1540s. After exile and cooperation with England's reformers, Knox returned to Scotland in the early 1560s when Mary, Queen of Scots (cousin of Queen Elizabeth) was beset with dynastic, domestic, and international crises. In a series of fierce interviews in 1562, Knox told the Catholic queen that he would continue to preach against her Catholic faith and would continue to insist on a thorough reformation of religious life in her kingdom. Mary would eventually run afoul of her Scottish and English rivals and be deposed in favour of her infant son James. Knox's leadership soon passed to Andrew Melville who was the major author of *The Second Book of Discipline* that outlined the Presbyterian church order that would dominate Scotland, with many political twists and major theological turns, for centuries thereafter.

England

England offers yet another story of a Protestant Christendom that was both successful and continually contested. In pursuit of strict uniformity in all aspects of religion, Queen Elizabeth sacked one of her archbishops of Canterbury for advocating his Calvinist theology too aggressively, she agreed to the execution of Catholic priests who stole back into England to serve the Catholic faithful, and she worked hard at restraining Protestants who pushed for further reform.

These advocates for a more complete Reformation eventually became known as Puritans – for their efforts to purify the English church of what they saw as vestigial Catholicism, but also for efforts at purifying the nation as a whole and individual believers in their private religious lives. In the late 16th century, leaders like Thomas Cartwright drew up plans for exchanging the inherited church order of bishops (Episcopalianism) for an order imitating Geneva's councils of ministers and lay elders (Presbyterianism). After Queen Elizabeth died in 1603 and was succeeded by her cousin James I, who had already been reigning north of the border as Scotland's James VI, many Puritan leaders advocated Congregationalism, which centred authority on local church assemblies.

Of the many long-lasting Puritan influences, one of the most important was a new stress on personal conversion. Earlier Protestants more or less took for granted the enfolding of individual believers into the corporate structures of Christendom. But in England, with the character of Christendom persistently contested, Puritans came to emphasize the need for a deliberate personal response to God's provision of salvation. The legacy for later born-again movements, especially among evangelical Protestants, was profound.

James I, who reigned until 1625, viewed Puritan proposals for reform as threats to his own authority. Early in his reign James convened a conference at Hampton Court where he allowed Puritan leaders to state their case for further reforms. With one exception, James would have none of it. When he heard their proposals to replace the authority of bishops with guidance from presbyteries or congregations, he responded sharply: 'No bishop, no king.' James expanded by saying that if he wanted to be menaced by a confusing mixture of church authorities he would have stayed in Scotland where a Presbyterian system prevailed.

The one exception was James' openness to the Puritans' request for a new translation of the Bible. As thorough Protestants devoted to Scripture, most Puritans had used an English translation made some decades earlier in Geneva by reformers driven out of England under the Catholic Queen Mary. James detested this version, however, because its translators had added marginal notes that in places called on believers to obey God and not kings. In this one instance, James' desire for a textually neutral Scripture and the Puritans' desire for an expansion of biblical literacy came together. The result was the Authorized, or King James, Version of the English Bible that was published in 1611 and that has exercised incalculable religious, linguistic, and literary influence ever since.

Mark 16:1–8 from the Authorized or King James Version (1611)

1 And when the sabbath was past, Mary Magdalene, and Mary the *mother* of James, and Salome, had bought sweet spices, that they might come and anoint him.

2 And very early in the morning the first *day* of the week, they came unto the sepulchre at the rising of the sun.

3 And they said among themselves, Who shall roll us away the stone from the door of the sepulchre?

4 And when they looked, they saw that the stone was rolled away: for it was very great.

5 And entering into the sepulchre, they saw a young man sitting on the right side, clothed in a long white garment; and they were affrighted.

6 And he saith unto them, Be not affrighted: Ye seek Jesus of Nazareth, which was crucified: he is risen; he is not here: behold the place where they laid him.

7 But go your way, tell his disciples and Peter that he goeth before you into Galilee: there shall ye see him, as he said unto you.

8 And they went out quickly, and fled from the sepulchre; for they trembled and were amazed: neither said they any thing to any *man*; for they were afraid.

When James' son, Charles I, succeeded to the throne in 1625, England's competing Christendoms moved from verbal combat, low-level insurgency, and sporadic repression to open war. Early in his reign, Charles gave signs of wanting to imitate the absolutist rule of the era's French monarchs and also to relax England's strictures against Roman Catholics. These moves spurred a coalition between his Parliamentary opponents, who feared the onset of despotism, and his Puritan opponents, who feared a retreat from the Reformation. A civil war beginning in 1642 was the result. During early stages of the conflict, reform-minded Protestants strongly supported the armies of Parliament against the Royalists. But then, as the broad Parliamentary–Puritan alliance gained the upper hand, internal dissension rent the coalition. English Presbyterians, English Congregationalists, and Scottish Presbyterians who had united against the king now attacked each other in efforts to refashion England's Christendom.

Among the leaders on the Parliamentary side, a few began to question the basic assumptions of the Christendom ideal. Richard Baxter, a chaplain in the parliamentary army and a notable parish minister, endured a series of unsettling ecclesiastical battles. As an antidote he urged differentiating between basic Christian convictions shared by most Protestants (and even some Catholics) and secondary concerns where differences of opinion did not have to be taken as seriously. Baxter's ideal of 'mere Christianity' has had a long and influential life, as illustrated most recently at the time of the Second World War when the British author C. S. Lewis took 'mere Christianity' as his theme for radio broadcasts and a bestselling book.

By far the most important leader to conceive new ways of organizing religion and society was the great parliamentary general, Oliver Cromwell. Cromwell, who after leading Parliament to victory on the field of battle became England's effective ruler from 1649 to 1658, remains a controversial figure. In his own day, he was a pariah in many parts of Europe for his role in putting King Charles I on trial and then pushing Parliament to execute the monarch in January 1649. Even greater obloquy has come in later centuries for his murderous assaults against Irish Catholics carried out as reprisals for earlier outrages against Irish Protestants. But Cromwell was also ahead of his times in believing that civil order did not require religious homogeneity. He is notable in the history of European Judaism for legalizing the readmission of Jews to England. And in both the Parliamentary Army and as Lord Protector he advocated a broad religious toleration (though excluding Catholics).

That toleration allowed unprecedented opportunities for several groups of Protestant Dissenters (so called for dissenting from the Anglican church-state establishment). Some of the most extreme, like the Ranters and the Muggletonians, quickly passed from the scene. But others, like the Baptists and the Society of Friends (Quakers), became permanent additions to the Protestant world.

The rise of the Baptists was particularly significant since they represented the sharpest challenge in England to the Christendom ideal. Baptists included both Calvinists, who stressed divine sovereignty in salvation, and Arminians, who followed the path of Jacob Arminius in giving more weight to the human role in redemption. Yet all of them reserved baptism for those who professed faith for themselves. Thus, they both harkened back to significant New Testament themes and anticipated the tide of individualism that was rising in Western law, commerce, ethics, and politics. Because they defended the right of the private interpretation of Scripture as a foundational Protestant principle, they made an unusually direct contribution to the growth of religious freedom understood in a modern sense. The division between those who practised adult-believer baptism and those who baptized infants remains an important rift within Protestantism, with definite implications for worship and social ideals as well as biblical interpretation.

In 1660, as exhausted by intra-Protestant religious strife as by political division, England restored the monarchy by calling Charles II, the son of Charles I, back from Europe. The Restoration led to an extreme recoil from anything associated with the Puritans. Yet the course of English Protestantism, as well as the English nation, had been decisively altered by the era's tumultuous events. The taste for religious toleration would eventually grow stronger; new forms of Protestant Dissent were well established; and the Puritan advocacy of a lively Calvinism personally appropriated left an enduring influence.

A mixed legacy

The era that stretched from the first Reformation generation to the renewal movements of the late 17th century was for Protestants the best of times and the worst of times. It was the best of times because the release of Protestant energies allowed Lutherans, the Reformed, and Anglicans to create local Christian civilizations that produced brilliant achievements with world-historical significance. It was the worst of times because these Protestant civilizations were continually embroiled in warfare, which opened the door to a godless secularism that was damaging for Christian convictions of all varieties.

Religious antagonism did not by itself create the dreadful run of wars and civil unrest that stretched from the 1540s to the 1650s. But it was everywhere an ingredient that drove differences to extremes and sanctioned the shedding of blood in God's name. The carnage multiplied in France during its Wars of Religion (1562–96) that pitted Catholics against Huguenots and that included many instances of savage treachery – most famously the St Bartholomew's Day Massacre of 1572 when Catholic mobs killed several thousand Protestants.

The long-lasting Revolt of the Netherlands that began in 1568 was sparked by the determination of Dutch Reformed Protestants to win independence from Catholic Spain, which was just as determined to maintain its rule. The mayhem of the English Civil War of the 1640s, as destructive as it was, paled besides the horrific slaughter of the Thirty Years War (1618–48). What began as a conflict between the Catholic Habsburgs and Protestants in Bohemia soon degenerated into military mayhem and callous butchery that devastated central Europe as it had not been devastated since the Black Death of the Middle Ages and would not be again until the First and Second World Wars.

As if the physical destruction of religious warfare was not monstrous enough, the European divisions exacerbated by competitive religious loyalties also made it easier for secularism to advance. With the rise of Protestantism and the end of the unified Western church – and, even more, with religion prominent in fomenting the devastation – more and more Europeans were ready to replace former Christian loyalties with allegiance to their particular nation states. The same circumstances stimulated some of Europe's most creative intellects to imagine lives liberated from the destructive guidance of any church.

A brighter side

The vision of Protestant Christendom that contributed to deadly European warfare also provided the intellectual depth and cultural scope for human creativity of an entirely different order. As an instance, Protestant art has never flourished as it did in the 17th and 18th centuries. Scholars debate the degree of Protestant influence in the late work of Albrecht Dürer (1471–1528) and in the paintings executed by Hans Holbein (1497–1543), like 'The Ambassadors', when he was employed by Protestant patrons in Switzerland and England. There is more consensus about the Reformed Protestant influences that shaped a later generation of world-class artists in the Netherlands. Jacob van Ruisdael (1628–82) painted evocative Dutch landscapes with little overt religious content, but they reflected his view of nature as a work of God, as explained in the Dutch Reformed

Belgic Confession of 1561: the divinely created 'universe is before our eyes like a beautiful book in which all creatures, great and small, are as letters to make us ponder the invisible things of God: his eternal power and his divinity'.

The height of Protestant artistry came with Rembrandt van Rijn (1606–69) whose life was marked by domestic trials and financial

4. Rembrandt van Rijn painted himself, with his wife Saskia, in this image of Jesus' parable of the Prodigal Son

embarrassments, but whose paintings have been sources of profoundest appreciation. In his mature works like *The Three Crosses*, *Abraham and Isaac*, or *The Return of the Prodigal*, Rembrandt offered intense and evocative, yet also restrained, visual mediations on the main narratives of the Christian gospels.

The 'Rembrandt' of music was Johann Sebastian Bach (1685–1750) who was employed by various cities and rulers in Germany before spending his last 27 years as the Kapellmeister in Saxon Leipzig. For his Lutheran employers, the cantatas, oratorios, masses, and organ preludes that poured from his mind matched music and text better than anyone has ever done in Christian history. For this strong-minded but also earnestly pious musician, however, even works without explicit religious content were composed, as he often wrote at the end of his compositions, S.D.G. (soli Deo Gloria, to the glory of God alone).

Bach's near-contemporary, George Frederick Handel (1685–1759), deployed more modern operatic techniques in his religious music, but compositions like *Messiah* also testified to the benefits arising from a society where culture and Christianity were taken for granted as mutually supporting partners.

George Herbert's 'The Agony'

George Herbert's great poem about the passion of Christ and the Eucharist (or Lord's Supper) was found after his death in 1633 as part of a manuscript called 'The Temple'. (Spelling is modernized slightly: 'behoove' means 'worthwhile'; 'sound' means 'explore'; and 'assay' means 'make an attempt'.)

> Philosophers have measur'd mountains,
> Fathom'd the depths of seas, of states, and kings,
> Walk'd with a staff to heav'n, and traced fountains:

> But there are two vast, spacious things,
> The which to measure it doth more behoove:
> Yet few there are that sound them; Sin and Love.
> Who would know Sin, let him repair
> Unto Mount Olivet; there shall he see
> A man so wrung with pains, that all his hair,
> His skin, his garments bloody be.
> Sin is that press and vice, which forceth pain
> To hunt his cruel food through ev'ry vein.
> Who knows not Love, let him assay
> And taste that juice, which on the crosse a pike
> Did set again abroach; then let him say
> If ever he did taste the like.
> Love is that liquor sweet and most divine,
> Which my God feels as blood; but I, as wine.

Literary products of English Christendom decorated 17th-century England with unusual brilliance. Readers through the centuries have recognized the different kinds of Protestant grounding that the high-church Anglican George Herbert brought to his metaphysical poetry (*The Temple*, published posthumously in 1633), the Puritan John Milton deployed with his distinctive theological accents in *Paradise Lost*, and in the Baptist John Bunyan's memorable story of a life's journey from the City of Destruction to the Celestial City (*Pilgrim's Progress*, 1678). Bunyan did write his great allegory while in jail for his Nonconformist convictions, but even in his case the capacity for large-minded literature depended on the common shared assumptions nurtured by England's formal Christian allegiance.

Chapter 3
Pietists, the American colonies, evangelicals, and the Enlightenment

In the century and a half between the Peace of Westphalia (1648) that ended the Thirty Years War and the rise of Napoleon (1790s), European Protestantism was revived, challenged, modified, repudiated, divided, and exported. During these years, the Protestant willingness to challenge received traditions strengthened. Sometimes, as with Unitarians, who abandoned traditional teaching on the Trinity, the new 'protests' meant changing inherited doctrines in accord with intellectual norms from the Enlightenment. More often it meant pietists or evangelicals seeking out new means to awaken spiritually tepid populations. Increasingly Protestants treated religious authority as something to be earned rather than bestowed. Most still upheld historic Christian teachings, but the creativity of Protestant movements in this period paralleled the era's innovations in colonial exploration, intellectual advance, and political consolidation.

Toward renewal

Although Pietism emerged in Europe as a definable movement of renewal only in the last decades of the 17th century, pietistic and evangelical emphases had been present long before. The first was a concentration on personal experience as the foundation for Christian life. That focus was exemplified powerfully in the reforming labours of Johann Arndt, a Lutheran pastor who worked in several different German cities. His much-reprinted *True Christianity*, published between 1605 and 1610, drew on elements of medieval spirituality like Thomas à Kempis' *Imitation of Christ* to urge personal appropriation of Christ and his work. Arndt's concern to enliven merely formal, notional, or tribal religion became the baseline for reforming efforts that continue to this day.

Such efforts also consistently returned for inspiration to the fountainhead of the Reformation. One ruler who looked explicitly to Martin Luther for the means to restore his territory after the great devastation of the Thirty Years War was Duke Ernst of Saxe-Gotha (1601–75), who became known as 'the Pious' for his reforming zeal. As the prime means for restoring his territory Ernst and his court chaplains zealously promoted Luther's 'Small Catechism' as their antidote to the crises of the age. For his efforts, Ernst was hailed as an exemplary Christian ruler by Oliver Cromwell and several more of the era's notable leaders.

As historian R. W. Ward has shown, movements of pietistic or evangelical renewal almost always emerged in response to political pressure from powerful states, such as those in the Habsburg empire, or powerful state-churches, both Protestant and Catholic. As a result, almost all renewal movements of the period entailed covert political protest alongside overt religious reform. So it was for Bohemian Lutherans holding out against the Catholic Habsburgs, pietists in central Europe protesting the rigidity of Lutheran and Calvinist state churches, and (later) reformers in Britain and its colonies struggling to lift the heavy weight of religious formalism.

Perhaps surprisingly, Protestant renewal movements also drew on older and more recent strands of Catholic spirituality. Pierre Poiret, a French-born author active among German and Dutch

Protestants, wrote several such works himself; he transcribed the visions of Antoinette Bourignon, a Flemish mystic who played down the era's strong divide between Catholics and Protestants; and he edited the works of Madam Jean de la Mothe Guyon, a Catholic quietist whose works inspired a wide range of Catholic and Protestant laypeople even as they worried church authorities for slighting church norms.

Pietism

On the continent, the key figure in what became known as Pietism was Philip Jakob Spener, pastor of Lutheran churches in Frankfurt am Main, Dresden, and Berlin. At Frankfurt in 1670, Spener instituted the *collegia pietatis* (or 'pious assembly'), a small group of laypeople who met on Wednesdays and Sundays in Spener's home to pray, discuss the previous week's sermon, and apply passages from Scripture and devotional writings to their lives. Such small groups would henceforth be a defining characteristic of Protestantism worldwide (as they are at Seoul's Yoido Full Gospel Church).

Spener's efforts reached a broader public when in 1675 he prepared a new preface for the published sermons of Johann Arndt. The preface was soon independently published as *Pia Desideria* (Pious Wishes); it created a sensation for its indictment of spiritual lethargy. Spener criticized nobles and princes for abusing their control over churches, ministers for substituting cold doctrine for warm faith, and laypeople for abandoning Luther's 'priesthood of all believers'. Spener's positive programme stressed fuller appropriation of Scripture, renewed dedication to day-in, day-out Christian practice, and ministerial training featuring spiritual life rather than polemical theology.

The proposals provoked both enthusiasm and opposition. Professional theologians were worried about their own authority and also about the danger of unchecked individual subjectivity.

Spener, who retained much traditional Lutheranism himself, rejected separatistic conclusions. But he was not always successful at keeping his most ardent followers from leaving the inherited churches. Neither did Spener's frequent appeals to Luther keep him from a subtle alteration of historic Reformation theology as he came to stress more the Christian's new birth (regeneration) than the traditional emphasis on the believer's right standing before God (justification).

The remainder of Spener's career was marked by controversy, but also successful recruitment of a capable successor. August Hermann Francke became the leading figure at the University of Halle that Spener had helped bring into existence in the early 1690s. Francke's labours at Halle – including, beside the university, schools for poor children, a world-famous orphanage, an institute for teacher training, a publishing house, and a pharmaceutical business with a worldwide clientele – became an inspiration for Protestants throughout Western society. Under his leadership, the University of Halle also became a missionary-training centre that pioneered in studying oriental languages and providing the tools for translating the Bible into non-Western languages.

The reforms sponsored by Spener and Francke soon multiplied into other varieties of German renewal in the early 18th century, the most important of which was the Moravians. In the early 1720s, a zealous, affable, but sometimes zany German Count, Ludwig Nicholas von Zinzendorf, welcomed refugees from Moravia (modern Czech Republic) to his estate in eastern Saxony. These Bohemian Brethren were descended from the 15th-century followers of Jan Hus. Zinzendorf, who was Spener's godson and Francke's student, organized the refugees into a kind of international *collegia pietatis*. These Moravians would soon carry the pietistic concern for personal spirituality almost literally around the world, with important missionary efforts in India, the West Indies, North America, and elsewhere. For the history of

English-speaking Christianity, it was of great significance that John Wesley was thrown into a company of Moravians during a voyage to Georgia in 1735. What he saw of their behaviour then and what he heard of their faith after returning to England contributed directly to his own evangelical awakening.

North American beginnings

Although European colonization in North America was multi-national and multi-religious from the start, the coming of British Protestantism exerted the decisive religious influence and led eventually to new forms of Protestant faith for the world. At first, however, Protestants in America tried simply to replicate what they had experienced in Europe by reconstituting Christendom in the colonies as they had known at home. Virginia, established in 1607, set up a parish Anglican system. Its leaders tried to exclude non-Anglicans even after the British Parliament passed a Toleration Act in 1689. Yet despite efforts by Anglicans in Virginia and the other southern colonies, the effort to transplant the English state church was foiled by parishes of immense size, persistent deficits of personnel and funds, and constant encroachment by Protestant Dissenters.

The middle colonies of New York, New Jersey, Pennsylvania, and Delaware, which were settled later, became home to a variety of Protestants almost from the start. Anglicans from England and Presbyterians from Scotland hoped to see some variation of the establishments they had known in Britain, but the early presence of Baptists and other English Dissenters made that impossible. By 1700, German Protestant migrants of several kinds had also arrived; even if they had come to the new world mostly with the desire to be left alone, they helped create a religious pluralism quite unusual for the age.

The founding of Pennsylvania made it even harder to think about importing Christendom to America. This proprietary colony belonged to the family of William Penn, son of a renowned English admiral who controlled a great tract of land spreading westward from the city of Philadelphia, which was laid out in 1682. Penn had been drawn to Quaker teachings as a young man and so tried to set up 'Penn's Woods' (that is, Pennsylvania) as an official Quaker colony, but one that also enshrined Quaker principles of religious freedom. The result was a 'Frame of Government' advancing an unprecedented degree of liberty to all who professed belief in One God. It put into practice what Penn had outlined in a path-breaking book published from 1670, *The Great Cause of Liberty of Conscience*. Penn's principled defence of religious freedom outlined the future for much of America, but it would not prevail until after the American Revolution of 1776. The difference from the old world was not the mere presence of such ideas, but that they shaped American civilization from the beginning.

The most impressive religious settlement in the New World was the work of Puritans in New England. This migration was another off-shoot of the conflicts between King and people that created England's Parliamentary-Puritan alliance of the 1620s and 1630s. While other English immigrants were only getting started, the New England Puritans succeeded in setting up a fully functioning Christian society. They were looking both backward and forward – backward, as the Puritans sought to construct a comprehensive Christendom in the new world; but also forward as they promoted notions of congregational autonomy and lay responsibility anticipating the freer Protestant forms of later American history.

Where Puritanism had flamed out as a society-shaping force in Britain after the collapse of Oliver Cromwell's Commonwealth in the late 1650s, New England Puritanism remained a cohesive reality into the 18th century and a source of cultural influence long thereafter. One of the reasons was the broader context. Disease had greatly reduced the Native American population as the settlers were arriving, and New England contained too few natural resources to be coveted by other European powers.

Effective leadership was just as important as the environment. In Massachusetts, the Rev. John Cotton preached a powerful message of divine grace, but also showed how those touched by grace could function together cohesively. His colleague, the Rev. Thomas Shepard, was appointed the minister in Cambridge because he ministered so effectively to the young men at the new Harvard College. Lay leadership was even more impressive. The primary leader of the Plymouth colony was William Bradford who guided this humble and less enterprising colony with unusual effectiveness. His counterpart in the wealthier and more ambitious Massachusetts Bay was John Winthrop who joined strong personal integrity to considerable political flexibility. (Plymouth and the Bay colony united in 1691.)

The American Puritans displayed their genius in the way they combined individual, ecclesiastical, and social connections. New Englanders asked prospective members to testify before the assembled congregation that they had undergone a saving experience of God's grace. Men and women who made this profession became church members; such a profession then entitled men to become freemen (or voters) in the colony. They used the biblical language of 'covenant' to describe relationships at each level. By having the covenants interlock, Puritans made vital personal religion political and kept colonial politics religious.

Under this general system the first generation of New England Puritans achieved considerable success. A few complaints did come from articulate protesters like Anne Hutchinson who asked provocatively why there had to be such tight regulation of churches and society if individuals really had received divine grace

Reformation. Wesley was a complex individual who was intermittently beset by doubts about his own standing before God. Yet he nonetheless succeeded in teaching a sophisticated Arminian theology (with more emphasis on freedom to choose or reject God than found in Calvinism), maintaining an aristocratic control of the Methodist movement as it expanded in the British Isles and eventually America, and preserving a sincere common touch in reaching out to ordinary laymen and laywomen.

Charles Wesley (1707–88) always lived in his brother's shadow, but as an indefatigable itinerant preacher and careful organizer he was almost as important as John in getting the Methodist movement underway. Yet his greatest contribution to the Methodist movement, and then to all of Christianity, was in hymnody. Many of his lifetime's 9,000 poems and hymns are forgettable, like those that excoriated the American colonists for seeking their independence from King George III or that lampooned the Wesleys' Calvinist opponents. But many others have given voice since they were written to the sincerest piety for Christian communities literally around the globe.

Charles Wesley's hymns

Many of Charles Wesley's hymns remain widely circulated to this day.

> 'And can it be that I should gain an interest in the Saviour's love'
> 'Arise my soul, arise'
> 'Christ, the Lord, is risen today'
> 'Christ, whose glory fills the skies'
> 'Come, thou long-expected Jesus'
> 'Hail the day that sees him rise'
> 'Hark, the herald angels sing'
> 'Jesus, lover of my soul'
> 'Lo, he comes with clouds descending'

> 'Love divine, all loves excelling'
> 'O, for a thousand tongues to sing'
> 'Rejoice, the Lord is king'
> 'Soldiers of Christ, arise'
> 'Ye servants of God, your master proclaim'

The Wesleys' friend, but also occasional theological opponent, was the most notable public speaker of his age, and perhaps of all British history. George Whitefield (1714–70) participated in a 'holy club' that Charles Wesley helped start at Oxford and then burst into public view as a preaching sensation. In the late 1730s, massive crowds of up to 20,000 assembled in London, British market towns, and eventually Scottish and colonial cities, to hear him proclaim the good news. While his theology was Calvinistic (hence his differences with the Wesleys), Whitefield preached so effectively that neither denominational nor theological boundaries constrained his influence. He was a master in setting out God's requirements for holiness and even more effective in depicting the work of Christ as the antidote for sin. Although he remained a Church of England clergyman throughout his life, both his pragmatic lack of concern for traditional church forms and his fierce dedication to preaching a general gospel message left a permanent legacy on all later evangelical movements.

The leading colonial supporter of the awakenings was Jonathan Edwards (1703–58) who pastored the Puritan Congregationalists of Northampton, Massachusetts, for more than two decades. From this post, he won renown for his own revival sermons; 'Sinners in the Hands of an Angry God' has been most often reprinted, even though Edwards more often preached on the beauties of Christ's grace and the harmony of the universe under God than on the graphic details of divine punishment. He was even more important for his writing that tried to discriminate between the ephemeral, often spectacular results of revival and the long-term, God-honouring effects that he defended as enduringly significant. Edwards was also a discriminating theologian and philosopher whose efforts at expressing historic Calvinist beliefs in the language of up-to-date philosophy have made him one of the most studied American religious thinkers of any time or place. But to indicate the turmoil brought by revivalistic forms of Christianity, Edwards' Northampton congregation in 1750 dismissed him from this pulpit.

From the start, news about evangelical experiences in particular places was passed on with great excitement to other interested parties in the North Atlantic region. In Scotland, Wales, Ireland, and England, concerned Protestants read about the experiences of Abigail Hutchinson of Northampton, Massachusetts, who on a Monday morning in 1735 was turned from despair and alienation to God. As her minister, Jonathan Edwards, explained the event, when 'these words came to her mind, "The blood of Christ cleanses from all sin" [they were] accompanied with a lively sense of the excellency of Christ, and his sufficiency to satisfy for the sins of the whole world. . . . By these things', Edwards concluded, Abigail 'was led into such contemplations and views of Christ, as filled her exceeding full of joy'.

Not long thereafter Protestants throughout the English-speaking world could read in the published journal of John Wesley what had befallen him at a small-group meeting organized by Moravians, who had recently come from the continent to England. It was on Wednesday, 24 May 1738, at the Moravian gathering on Aldersgate Street in London,

> where one was reading Luther's preface to the *Epistle to the Romans*. About a quarter before nine, while he was describing the change which God works in the heart through faith in Christ, I felt my heart strangely warmed. I felt I did trust in Christ, Christ alone for salvation; and an assurance was given me that He had taken

away *my* sins, even *mine*, and saved *me* from the law of sin and death.

Many English-speaking Protestants followed just as closely reports concerning the great crowds that came out to hear George Whitefield as he travelled through Britain and North America and then of the extraordinary revival at Cambuslang, near Glasgow in Scotland, which began in February 1742 and continued for several months.

The public preaching of repentance and free grace, new institutions arising to perpetuate that message, hymns expanding its effects, and experiences like those of Abigail Hutchinson and John Wesley constituted the origins of the evangelical movement.

Protestants and the Enlightenment

Pietists and evangelicals were theologically conservative in embracing main doctrines of traditional Protestantism. But they were also modernizing as they used up-to-date techniques and took for granted a contemporary sense of the self as they proclaimed the Christian message. As such, some of their emphases overlapped with main currents of the era's broader intellectual movements that historians call the Enlightenment. Although these movements led some Europeans to more secular, or even atheistic, conclusions, for most Protestants the ordinary pattern was for selective appropriation.

Enlightenment notions of human intellectual capacity, the superiority of reason to church traditions, and the inevitability of human progress were most evident among advanced religious thinkers on the continent, the Moderate party in the Scottish church, and latitudinarian Anglicans in Britain. As they stressed the reasonableness of religion and the advantages of broad (= latitudinarian) toleration for divergent theological perspectives, these thinkers were more willing than most of their peers to question traditional beliefs about the unique authority of Scripture and to propose that all people of good will in whatever religious tradition could be found pleasing to God. Under such influences, convictions that had once been considered heretical gained a foothold among some Protestants. Universalists read the Scriptures to say that all humanity would in the end be redeemed. Questions about the Trinity multiplied in learned circles, with a few cautious critics advancing the Unitarian conclusion that denied the Trinity outright. By the end of the 18th century, Deism appeared as a general belief in one God but a denial of miracles and much else in traditional Christianity. (Benjamin Franklin, Tom Paine, and Thomas Jefferson were among the notables of the period whose religion resembled Deism.)

It would be wrong, however, to think that Enlightenment and traditional Protestant commitments were mutually exclusive. Some of the era's leading theologians took very seriously the advances made by Sir Isaac Newton and other natural philosophers (scientists). Jonathan Edwards in colonial Massachusetts and the Anglican Bishop George Berkeley, for instance, proposed slightly different accounts of God's all-encompassing mind as the foundation of reality; their aim was to exploit contemporary Enlightenment advances while preserving traditional understandings of God's character and actions. Their contemporary, the Anglican Bishop Joseph Butler, argued in his famous *Analogy of Religion, Natural and Revealed* (1736) that the picture of the world delivered by the best contemporary science was so closely analogous to the picture of morality and providence developed in Scripture, it was reasonable as well as pious to conclude that God was the controlling author of both.

Even more common interconnections are illustrated by Philip Jakob Spener and John Wesley, who often accentuated for Christian purposes many of the same currents that also defined the Enlightenment. Thus, Spener and Wesley – like spokesmen for the Enlightenment and in opposition to the established churches – were self-conscious innovators who readily gave up traditions that struck them as out-of-date; they laid great stress on testing the reality of faith by its 'experimental' (or experiential) nature rather than on its conformity with tradition; they were intensely interested in practical, even utilitarian, effects of faith, rather than merely conformity to inherited truths; and they made the action of the individual critical for the life of faith as opposed to stressing dictates handed down from the previous generation. In such ways, Spener and Wesley promoted a form of Christianity that partook of the Enlightenment, even though their purposes were explicitly Christian.

Chapter 4
Flourishing, flailing, fragmenting

Churches in Europe reeled from a double blow at the start of the 19th century. In the centre of Europe, leaders of the French Revolution of 1789 ruthlessly attacked Catholicism in their general assault on France's *ancien régime*. By extension, the Revolutionaries' slogan of 'liberty, equality, fraternity' was just as threatening to hereditary European Protestantism. In addition, as the armies of Napoleon emerging from the tumult of the French Revolution conquered more and more of Europe, they dismantled long-standing traditions of church and state cooperation extending back to the Reformation era and beyond. The result was a crisis of European Christendom.

In North America, there was a different kind of crisis. On a continent of vast physical space, a small but overwhelmingly Protestant population of European descent was struggling to set up Christian institutions and instill Christian moral values, but without the usual supports of Christendom. The new United States, which declared its independence in 1776, soon thereafter moved decisively to separate church and state. Practically, too, many kinds of Christianity were represented among the European settlers to establish any one of them. In addition, America's strong contingent of Dissenting Protestants defended religious liberty as a God-given right. To European Christians, the American experiment seemed doomed to fail since nothing like it had ever been attempted in European history before.

The North American difference

Two developments became especially important for North American Protestants, but also for the long-term history of Protestantism worldwide. As best explained in the writings of the historian–theologian Andrew Walls, the first was the successful adaptation of traditional European Christianity to the liberal social environment of the United States. The second was the emergence of the voluntary society as the key vehicle for Protestant organization.

Voluntary organization adapted to a free-market culture fueled one of the most dramatic expansions that to that time had ever taken place in the long history of Christianity. From 1815 to 1914, the US population grew very rapidly (from 8,400,000 to 99,100,000). Yet over the same century, attachment to the churches grew even faster, from under one-fourth of the population to over two-fifths as formal church members or regular adherents. Only the recent history of Christianity on the continent of Africa and in China reveals a more rapid increase of Christian adherents in a single geographical location.

Crucial for this expansion was the voluntary, self-directed exploitation of a liberal social order. American Protestants formed their own churches and religious agencies, generated their own financial support, and relied on themselves to teach and spread their faith. The older state-churches of Europe (Catholics, Episcopalians, Presbyterians, Lutherans, English Puritan Congregationalists) adjusted rapidly to the new American pattern, if only to keep pace with representatives of Europe's Dissenting traditions (Quakers, Baptists, Unitarians), and the newer Protestant movements of the modern period (Methodists and many newly created groups).

FRANCIS ASBURY
1745 — 1816
PIONEER
METHODIST BISHOP

6. Although this statue of Francis Asbury is prominently placed in Washington, DC, most of his life-long travels were in the byways of the American frontier

The leader of early American Methodism, and one of the most important figures in American history, was Francis Asbury. Born of English working-class stock, Asbury was dispatched by John Wesley in 1771 to assist the fledgling Methodist movement in the colonies. Immediately he began the itinerations that would carry him over 300,000 miles, mostly on horseback, before his death in 1816. When Methodists in the new United States gathered at Christmas in 1784 to regularize their status in relationship to Wesley, Asbury was both elected (by his American peers) and appointed (by Wesley) as bishop. Asbury was neither a compelling preacher like George Whitefield nor a creative theologian like Wesley, but he combined abilities that made him a perfect leader for a new religious movement in a vast and underpopulated land. He preached fervently on central gospel texts, he avoided entangling political involvement, he personally recruited several thousand young men to join him as itinerants, he organized the Methodist Discipline efficiently that gave itinerants their assignments and coordinated larger gatherings of the faithful, and he outmanoeuvred opponents who jeopardized the movement with unrestrained commitment to democratic ideology. Under Asbury, the Methodists demonstrated how well organized and effective a Christian church could become without the supports of Christendom.

Remnants of the Christendom ideal did, however, remain; for example, when tax-supported public education took off in the 1830s and 1840s, most schools prescribed daily readings from the Protestant King James Bible and took for granted the need to inculcate Protestant moral values. But the Protestant churches nonetheless embodied a much more informal Christianity and pushed consistently for ever-more flexible institutions and ever-newer innovations in responding to spiritual challenges.

That flexibility was manifest in the ease with which new churches could spring to life in this fertile environment. Among the most important was a new movement coordinated by a Dissenter from Scotland, Alexander Campbell, and a former Presbyterian, W. Barton Stone. Campbell and Stone were both inspired by the dynamism of the primitive church as described in the Book of Acts and also enthralled by the vision of personal liberty coming from the American Revolution. Stone was a particularly effective revival preacher, Campbell an unusually gifted polemicist and editor. Their movement, which they insisted be called simply 'Christians', came together in 1832. The church bodies arising from this Restorationist Movement (Church of Christ, Christian Church, Disciples of Christ) became enduring representatives of Dissenting Protestantism merged with freedom-loving American ideals.

The Church of Jesus Christ of Latter-day Saints (or Mormons) represented an American creation further from traditional Protestant norms. The Book of Mormon that its prophet, Joseph Smith, promulgated as an extension of biblical revelation became the foundation of first a new civilization in the western American desert of Utah and then the stimulus for a new church that has spread around the world.

Out of a welter of related movements driven by speculations about the end of the world came another American original, Seventh-day Adventism, which has gradually evolved closer to traditional Protestantism. A sea captain with connections to the Restorationist movement, Joseph Bates (1792–1872), and visionary Ellen G. White (1827–1915) helped found a church that produced health reformers (including the Kellogg family of breakfast cereal fame), stressed the importance of religious freedom, and argued from Scripture that the Christian day of worship should remain the Old Testament Sabbath (that is, Saturday). Over the last century, the Seventh-day Adventists has been one of the most effective missionary organizations in all of Christian history. Today their congregations are found in over 200 countries, or more than any other Protestant denomination.

Alexis de Tocqueville explained American distinctiveness to Europeans in a landmark book, *Democracy in America* (1835/1840) that was published after an extensive North American tour: the United States, he wrote, is the place in the world where the Christian religion has most preserved genuine powers over souls; and nothing shows better how useful and natural to man it is in our day, since the country in which it exercises the greatest empire is at the same time the most enlightened and most free.

Tocqueville was highlighting the elective affinity between a conversionistic, voluntaristic form of Christianity and a fluid, rapidly changing, commerce-driven, insecure, and ethnically pluralistic society. In turn, this new American pattern rather than European Christendom eventually became the model for Protestant development in the world as a whole.

Churches, society, and politics

Beginning with the changes propelled by Napoleon's armies, the nation state increasingly became Europe's central institution to which populations looked for the security, public order, and intellectual guidance once provided by the churches. Growing concentrations of state power also led to destructive international warfare that the churches proved unable, and sometimes unwilling, to restrain.

The heavy hand of state interference could be applied directly. In 1817, the King of Prussia, Frederick William III, forced the Lutheran and Reformed (or Calvinist) churches of his realm into an unwilling Union. Bitter theological quarrels between pietistic-leaning and modern- or scientific-leaning factions also weakened the cultural authority of the remaining Lutheran state churches, even as similar partisan differences divided Anglicans into high church (Anglo-Catholic), low church (evangelical), and broad church (liberal) factions. The 19th-century schisms among Dutch Reformed and Scottish Presbyterians testified to the feisty vigour of the splintering factions but also undercut the churches' general authority in these Calvinist countries.

During the first half of the 19th century, the most important achievement of Protestant social activism was the abolition of slavery. Led by William Wilberforce, a British evangelical aristocrat, and a dedicated band of Quaker philanthropists, slow but steady progress in arguing for the incompatibility of slavery with either Christianity or modern civilization led Britain to end the slave trade in 1807 and abolish the institution entirely in 1833. Wilberforce's broader efforts at encouraging privileged classes to lead Britain in practising godliness were never entirely successful, and Wilberforce himself was mostly blind to hardships among the working poor caused by the Industrial Revolution. But he did pave the way for others who tried to christianize Britain's rapidly industrializing social order.

At the start of the 19th century, the Quaker Elizabeth Fry was an effective pioneer for a humane prison system. In Scotland, the Presbyterian Thomas Chalmers proposed a much-noticed system of home visitations in his teeming Glasgow that, though ultimately not successful in overcoming urban poverty, was much admired at home and abroad. Some social conservatives who upheld the political status quo also became effective reformers. Of these the most hard-working was Anthony Ashley Cooper (the seventh Earl of Shaftesbury, 1801–85) who campaigned on behalf of the mentally ill, supported broader educational opportunities, and tried to regulate the hours that women and children worked in factories. Towards the end of the century, William (1829–1912) and Catherine (1829–90) Booth founded the Salvation Army as a vehicle for addressing a whole range of urban social needs while still vigorously promoting their Holiness vision of the gospel. Also at the end of the century, Keir Hardy (1856–1915), a founder of Britain's socialist Labour Party, drew some inspiration from dissenting Protestant convictions for his work on behalf of women's suffrage and for reform of the work place.

In the United States, where socialism was never considered seriously as a political option, Protestant voluntary societies pursued reforms in education, prison reform, temperance, and anti-slavery. As successful as some of these efforts were, slavery and racial prejudice against people of African descent created special problems in creating a Christian civilization. The disposition to regard slavery as a private concern fit all too well with the energetic, but also strongly individualistic character of the American Protestant mood.

The United States' bloody Civil War from 1861 to 1865 was, thus, a religious as well as political crisis. Some northern Protestants felt they had a God-given mandate to end slavery. White southern Protestants felt even more strongly that Scripture allowed for this institution. Neither side was willing to challenge assumptions about African American inferiority that the churches did little to dispel.

The post-war adjustment to rapid industrialization and urbanization was almost as disquieting, since Protestants who had mastered social and political life in rural and small-town America seemed over-mastered by the realities of large-scale manufacturing, mass-market commerce, and urban popular culture. One woman who simply got on with reforming efforts was an energetic Methodist, Frances Willard, who led the Women's Christian Temperance Union; its goal was to reduce alcohol abuse and thereby help the women and children who were so often the casualties of drunkenness. A parallel movement with broader ambitions, but less immediate success, was called the Social Gospel. Its most prominent spokesman, the German–American Walter Rauschenbusch, drew on his own experiences as a pastor in a New York slum and concentrated study of the Hebrew prophets to call for Protestant leadership in meeting the needs of urban America.

Only rarely in responses to the challenges of modern commercial and industrial life did Protestantism produce a leader like Abraham Kuyper of the Netherlands. Kuyper was a perpetual motion machine who as theologian, politician, educator, churchman, and editor grasped instinctively that the comprehensive challenges of modernity required comprehensive Christian responses. His efforts to enliven Calvinists with piety and stiffen revivalists with Calvinism led to practical mobilization of ordinary citizens; his movement addressed problems in labour, industry, education, and politics with comprehensive religious principles. Kuyper's ideas would go on to have impact elsewhere in the world where Dutch Calvinists settled. Yet even his admirers conceded that it was easier to lay out comprehensive Christian plans than to shape an entire society, as Kuyper discovered in his one, only moderately successful term as the Dutch prime minister (1901–5).

Theology, Scripture, and science

From the late 18th century, Protestants faced mounting challenges to the historic anchorage of Western culture in Christian faith. The great philosophical influences of the period – like Immanuel Kant and G. W. F. Hegel in Germany, J. S. Mill in Britain, and Karl Marx in his peripatetic life – laboured to replace traditional dependence upon revelation and religious traditions with what they held were more secure foundations in human reason, utilitarian calculation, or liberation of the means of production.

Immanuel Kant's challenge

Immanuel Kant offered a forthright challenge to traditional Protestants (and also Catholics) in *Religion within the Limits of Religion Alone* (1793):

> [T]rue religion is to consist not in the knowing or considering of what God does or has done for our salvation but in what we must do to become worthy of it....and of whose necessity every man can become wholly certain without any Scriptural learning whatever....Man *himself* must make or have made himself into whatever, in a moral sense, whether good or evil, he is or is to become.

The most thorough effort to adjust inherited faith to the metaphysical challenges of modernity came from the German theologian F. D. E. Schleiermacher. In 1799, he published a series of lectures entitled *Religion: Speeches to Its Cultured Despisers*. This book, and a lifetime of influential theologizing that followed, retained more emphases from Schleiermacher's pietist upbringing than his critics were sometimes willing to concede. But by moving the heart of Christianity toward 'God-consciousness', or more generally to 'a sense of dependence', Schleiermacher opened the way for radical redefinitions of the faith in terms of human aspirations, human perceptions, and human-felt needs.

A different kind of response was proposed by an intensely whimsical Danish Lutheran, Søren Kierkegaard (1815–55). While mounting the most rigorous intellectual critique of his age's dominant philosophical fashions, Kierkegaard anticipated some aspects of modern existentialism. In his provocative defence of Christianity, he insisted that dogma must be lived out in daily practice as the only way to overcome the force of post-Christian thinking and the even more deadly peril of Christian complacency.

Protestant theology in the 19th century was also marked by a growing chasm between innovative work enlisting broad popular support and the specialized studies of the academy. The climax of broadly liberal academic theology was reached in lectures published by Adolf von Harnack of Berlin in 1900. Entitled *What Is Christianity?*, they contended that the simple gospel preached by Jesus had been largely lost when it was translated into a Hellenistic idiom. Harnack, an immensely learned scholar whose historical works on the early centuries of Christianity are still read with profit, felt that the simple original gospel could be summarized as the Fatherhood of God, the Brotherhood of Man, and the infinite value of the human soul.

Such views made little headway among the Protestant populace at large. Those arenas were much more attuned to the theories of

John Nelson Darby, one of the founders of the Christian (or Plymouth) Brethren movement. After Darby broke from his early association with the Anglican Church of Ireland, his teaching about the separate 'dispensations' of Scripture and his particular explanation of biblical prophesy enjoyed a broad following. It was the same with several parties within Methodism who worked to keep alive John Wesley's ideal of holiness. An especially popular advocate of these views was the American Phoebe Palmer who set them forth in a much-read book, *The Way of Holiness* (1843). Palmer was also notable in her day for defending the right of women to preach in public. The Holiness movement that Palmer and like-minded teachers promoted advanced biblical interpretations that would later develop into Pentecostalism.

Throughout the 19th century, Protestant divisions on questions of Scripture continued to multiply. Earlier it had been differences over what the Bible taught that produced division; now questions about the character of Scripture itself were also a source of contention. As the tendency gained momentum in academic circles to picture the Bible as a human text subject to ordinary processes of historical development, Protestants divided sharply in response. Many popular voices simply rejected the new 'higher criticism', but rarely with much intellectual depth. A few well-trained scholars, like William Robertson Smith (1846–94) of the Free Church of Scotland, tried to show that newer conceptions of biblical interpretation could strengthen rather than undercut confidence in the main Christian message. The long church trials that Smith endured in the Free Church showed that this combination of commitments would be a tough sell in a Protestant world increasingly polarized between church and academy.

At the end of the 19th century, a trio of English biblical scholars showed what could still be done by traditional Christians who exploited the era's most formidable learning. The 'Cambridge

Triumverate' – Brooke Foss Westcott, Joseph Barber Lightfoot, and Fenton J. A. Hort – expertly deployed classical and contemporary learning to demonstrate the basic integrity of the New Testament text and the general reliability of sub-apostolic history. By so doing, they defused much of the alarm at the startling eurekas of contemporary biblical criticism.

Despite the intrinsic merit of work such as that carried out by the Cambridge scholars, all who compared the 19th-century situation to what had existed earlier realized that things had greatly changed. If it had become necessary to *defend* the divine character of Scripture, the Christendom that once had given total (if often inattentive) loyalty to the Bible was losing its hold.

Challenges from the study of nature came to a head with Charles Darwin's *Origin of Species* (1859). His account of biological evolution over immense eons caused by the accumulation of minute variations posed difficulties for traditional interpretations of the Bible, and Protestants divided on how to respond. Some chose to defend early Genesis as a literal account of how God made the world. Others adjusted their understanding of Scripture to fit the new evolutionary schemes. By the end of the 19th century, a few conservative Protestants, like the learned Benjamin B. Warfield of Princeton Theological Seminary, developed a middle position with considerable nuance. It held that God had created the world and the human soul by direct acts and also providentially supervised all other physical phenomena; but it looked to scientific research for explanations of how the phenomena may have evolved. This picture was too conservative for some Protestants and too liberal for others. Moreover, a new class of professional scientists employed by governments and universities was working energetically to show why their systematic research qualified them to replace amateur naturalists, many of whom clergymen, as the definitive authorities on what the natural world was really like.

Religious life

As consequential as issues of science and theology had grown over the course of the century, the broadest and deepest challenges were economic, cultural, and social. When citizens moved into the cities and found either improved economic prospects or harsh poverty, older religious habits suffered. The ability of more people to buy more manufactured goods opened the way to a fuller life, but also allowed fixation on consumption to push aside prayer, church attendance, family worship, and private devotion. For the vastly increased numbers of the new urban poor, poverty, disease, and the break-up of families were even more harmful. In America, opportunities for getting ahead often upset steady Christian adherence; throughout the 19th century, European visitors marveled at the energy of Americans but also wondered what constant pursuit of the dollar would do to Christian faith.

If, however, urban life created new problems, it also provided new opportunities, especially for organized revival. In Scandinavia, the Danish Lutheran minister and hymn writer Nikolai Grundtvig and especially the Norwegian layman Hans Nielsen Hauge established networks of revival that were supported by 'prayer houses' within the Lutheran churches. To this day descendents of those networks offer unusual support for several long-lived missionary ventures.

In Scotland, the brothers Robert and James Alexander Haldane, who were both converted in 1795 amid great worries about an invasion from France, went on to promote revival and missions in Scotland, England, France, Switzerland, and around the world. Their work had some influence on another pair of brothers, the Frenchmen Frédéric and Adolphe Monod, who were prime movers behind *Le Réveil* that energized the Reformed Protestant churches in France and Switzerland. Izaak da Costa of the Netherlands was one of the most interesting promoters of renewal, for he was not only an able apologist who wrote against modernist theology, but also a much-read poet whose poems reached a wide audience.

The Anglo-Saxon world enjoyed a number of comparably prominent public preachers. The converted American attorney Charles Finney captivated audiences in America and Britain with preaching marked by lawyerly logic, moral earnestness, and a rational understanding of the divine – human relationship. His *Lectures on Revival* (1835) was a bestseller in his own day and later became a much-read manual for newer Protestant regions of the world.

Urban revivalism reached new levels of popularity after mid-century, especially because of the effective ministry of Dwight L. Moody. This plain-speaking layman became famous in America only after a well-publicized tour of England and Scotland in the early 1870s. Until his death in 1899, Moody's skilful mix of Bible stories and homey illustrations, as well as an ability to work with a wide range of subgroups, made him the most visible Protestant figure of the era. His effectiveness was much increased through a long and fruitful partnership with Ira Sankey, the first popular revival song-leader and a highly successful publisher of gospel songs. In an era increasingly influenced by commercialized popular culture, Sankey used his musical abilities creatively, but in the time-honoured Protestant pattern of adjusting Christian proclamation to the popular tastes of mass audiences. The downside of revival in the Moody–Sankey mode was its increasing distance from the real-life problems of industrial society.

Less spectacular than the revivalists, but with greater influence in specific locales were the era's many 'princes of the pulpit'. Their epitome was Charles Haddon Spurgeon (1834–92) of London's Metropolitan Tabernacle. A self-trained Baptist of Calvinist conviction, Spurgeon's careful but accessible weekly sermons drew throngs to his church; in their published form these sermons have sold continuously from that day to this.

The 19th century was another great age of Protestant hymnody, but this time with female hymn writers in the lead. Hymn-writing had been one of the first venues opened for public female contributions to Protestant life, with the English Baptist Anne Steele, the author of several long-popular hymns (like 'Father, Whate'er of Earthly Bliss') as an 18th-century pacesetter. By the early 19th century, popular literature afforded further opportunities. The extraordinary output of tracts and popular texts from Hannah More contributed measurably to the rising influence of evangelical Anglicanism in the early decades of the century.

The women hymn writers of the 19th century included one genius at translation, Catherine Winkworth. She was more responsible than any one else for bringing the riches of Lutheran, Moravian, and other Germany hymnody to the English-speaking world. Better known as authors in their own right were the Anglican Charlotte Elliott ('Just as I am without one plea, but that thy blood was shed for me'), the Swedish Lutheran Lina Sandell ('Children of the Heavenly Father'), and the blind American Fanny Crosby ('Rescue the Perishing' and 'To God be the glory').

By the end of the 19th century, two general matters had become obvious in the larger Protestant world. The new realities of Western industrial society were beginning to ease Protestants out of the central role they had long enjoyed. But the Protestant world still possessed spiritual energy of unusual vitality. With more than enough hopes, duties, and fears on the home front, almost no one in 1900 could have foreseen the great changes in the wider world that were soon to revolutionize Protestant history.

Chapter 5
Missionary transformations

The great transformation that made Protestantism into a worldwide Christian movement began with German pietists in the late 17th century. Although early Protestant theologies stressed the universality of the good news of Christ (the gospel), the first generations concentrated on what the gospel could do for Europeans. Geopolitics largely explains why Protestants were slow in launching missionary ventures. For all world religions, most missionary work has been undertaken in relationship with international trade, colonial expansion, or the diasporic movement of peoples. The expanding European powers of the early Protestant years were Catholic – Portugal, Spain, and then France.

Only in the 17th century, when Protestant nations like the Netherlands and England began to extend their sway over the seas, did interest grow in bringing Christianity to non-Europeans. Reformed ministers from Holland, who in the 17th century were sent out to serve colonial officials of the Dutch East India Company, shared the Christian faith with residents of Java (modern Indonesia) and Taiwan. After the New England Puritan John Eliot was installed as pastor to English colonists in Roxbury, Massachusetts, he began serious missionary outreach to nearby Iroquois Indians. Eliot's translation of the Bible into Algonquian (New Testament, 1661; Old Testament, 1663) was especially noteworthy for illustrating the basic Protestant commitment to

Scripture and for anticipating the great translation efforts that would mark later Protestant history. Yet for Eliot and the Dutch, the spread of Christianity remained an adjunct of colonial expansion. In both of these cases, preliminary success at gathering new converts was later undone by warfare, conflict with other European powers, and exploitative colonial policy.

When renewal movements within continental Lutheranism led to cross-cultural missions that escaped the imperatives of colonial expansion, a momentous new stage in world Protestant history began to emerge. Compared to Catholic missions, Protestant efforts were less centralized and considerably more likely to spin off indigenous local expressions. The transformation that would eventually lead to a widely dispersed, highly diverse, and strongly multicultural world Protestantism began in India in the early 18th century with a blueprint drawn up at the German pietist centre in Halle.

India as pattern

Bartholomäus Ziegenbalg and Heinrich Plütschau were the missionaries who arrived in 1706 at Tranquebar, on the south-eastern coast of the India subcontinent, with goals that had been formulated by August Herman Francke in Prussian Halle. Historian Robert Frykenberg has specified the vision that had already stimulated Protestant renewal in Europe and that was now poised to reshape the world:

> Christian obedience to the Great Commission [a reference to Matthew 28:19–20], if taken seriously, required that every single soul on earth, whether child or adult, male or female, should have a continuous personal access to the Word of God; and that each should be enabled to read in her or his own mother tongue.

The back story of this missionary effort illustrates the importance of European politics. It involved King Frederick IV of Denmark (reigned 1699–1730) who had been won over to Francke's vision and so offered his small imperial holdings in India as a base for missionary work. Frederick's cousin, Queen Anne of England (reigned 1702–14), was also an important patron of early missionaries. As princess and then queen, she supported the first organized efforts at Anglican activity overseas, the Society for Promoting Christian Knowledge (SPCK) and the Society for the Propagation of the Gospel (SPG). Cooperation between the reform-minded monarchs was crucial for the missionaries who went out to India, since the early British and Danes already present in India, especially representatives of Britain's East India Company, regularly obstructed missionary efforts. Where the missionaries sought souls, they wanted profits.

Although Ziegenbalg died after only thirteen years in India, his extraordinary career foreshadowed the best of later efforts. As soon as he arrived, he applied himself to learn the local languages; he collected the hand-written texts in which Tamil literature then existed; within a year he set up an 'orphan school' (modeled on Francke's Halle orphanage) for the instruction of non-elite Indian children; he trained Tamil teachers and pastors and gave them authority for new churches and new schools; he wrote lengthy letters back to Germany describing everything he saw; he set to work translating the Bible (New Testament, 1715; Old Testament after his death); and he imported type with other necessary equipment from Germany so that he could print Christian and other literature in Tamil.

After Ziegenbalg's untimely death, he was succeeded by other far-sighted pietist missionaries. The most remarkable was Christian Friedrich Schwartz, who served in India from 1750 to 1798. With his facility in at least five Indian languages, Schwartz combined the intellectual curiosity of the Enlightenment with pietist Christian zeal. He worked with the Anglican SPCK, functioned as a chaplain to European colonists, extended schooling to many Indians, commissioned native Christian workers, carried out diplomatic missions between the British and Indian rulers, and organized relief when famine struck.

Yet the most important factor in the spread of Protestantism in India was always the work of Indians themselves. Very early in Ziegenbalg's career he recruited Ganapati Vattiyar, an accomplished Tamil poet, as his partner in scholarship and evangelization. As famous as C. F. Schwartz became as a European expert on all things Indian, his long-term impact was greatest through the 'Helpers (*Upadesiars*) of God' whom he recruited to nurture Indians in Christian faith. These 'Helpers' included at least one Maratha Brahman widow, Royal Clorinda, who enlisted Schwartz's aid in founding a charity school and a prayer hall. The 'Helpers' were so widely respected that some local Indian potentates, like the Maharaja of Thanjavur, Serfoji, turned to them for models of justice and standards of education. Schwartz's best-known disciple was Vedanayakam Sastriar, son of a high caste Tamil Christian poet, who became superintendent of the main school in the Maharaja Serfoji's Thanjavur principality. Vedanayakam mastered Tamil literature, both classical and modern, and in so doing illustrated the capacity of Christianity in an indigenized form to take root in cultural soil far from Europe.

The pattern of transmission that in less than a century led from Francke's vision in Halle to Indian-led churches with thousands of Indian adherents was the pattern that made Protestantism into a world religion. In the centuries since Vedanayakam Sastriar flourished, the pattern has often been disrupted by Western colonists and merchants exploiting, abusing, or dismantling local cultures. Conflicts between adherents to other deities and the new Christian god, as well as native loyalty to ancestral religions, have also confounded dreams of Christian evangelization. Especially damaging to the development of self-standing local Protestant churches was the high tide of European colonial expansion – at its peak from about 1875 to 1960 – when Westerners most aggressively tried to organize the world for their own purposes.

But local appropriation was always most important for the long term. Without the local choice to embrace the Christian faith for local reasons, the great movement of the Christian churches outside of the Western world simply would not have taken place.

Innovations

The channels through which Protestantism broke out of settled Western ways multiplied in the century after the Lutheran pietists left Germany. Hard on their heels came the Moravians. From a modern perspective, the Moravians were by far the most attractive early Protestant missionaries. They came very close to being apolitical; they were eager to learn native languages and learn about local cultures; they avoided colonizing violence; and they preached a gospel message stressing God's love for all humans. Moravian missionaries began to stream out of Count von Zinzendorf's estate in Saxony from 1732 onwards. Missionaries like David Nitschmann were soon at work among slaves in St Thomas of the Virgin Islands. David Zeisberger did similar work among the Delaware Indians in eastern Pennsylvania even as he helped to establish a Moravian settlement at Bethlehem in the same colony. Zinzendorf and his successor, August Gottlieb Spangenberg, trotted the globe to encourage missionaries, strengthen Moravian settlements, and raise money. Very soon, converts like Rebecca Protten, a slave on St Thomas who was eventually freed and later married a Moravian missionary, themselves became effective evangelists. Moravian successes were sometimes short-lived, due sometimes to their own failures (Zinzendorf was a notoriously poor administrator) and sometimes to circumstances beyond their control (like the attacks on peaceful Indian converts in Pennsylvania during the French and Indian, or Seven Years, Wars). Yet in their 18th-century labours and in the Moravian communities that exist to this day throughout the world, they have been among the Protestant missionaries who come closest to the high ideals of the Christian gospel.

Other Protestants of the era were also pushing hard against the boundaries of Christendom. They included the first converted slaves in North America to become active church leaders. Missionaries sponsored by the Anglican SPG and the Calvinistic Puritans of New England had made some largely ineffective attempts to evangelize enslaved African Americans. The first general interest in Christianity among North America's growing slave population was not sparked, however, until the colonial Awakenings of the 1740s. Its leaders, like George Whitefield, did not attack the institution of slavery itself, but they did preach a message of spiritual liberation that attracted many converts.

Jupiter Hammon

The first publication of any kind by an African American appeared in 1760; it was a poem by the life-long slave Jupiter Hammon (c. 1711–c. 1805) entitled 'An Evening Thought: Salvation by Christ, with Penetential [sic] Cries'. Here are 5 of the poem's 22 stanzas.

Salvation comes by Christ alone,
The only Son of God;
Redemption now to every one,
That love his holy Word....
Dear Jesus, give thy Spirit now,
Thy Grace to every Nation,
That han't [hasn't] the Lord to whom we bow,
The Author of Salvation.
Ho! every one that hunger hath,
Or pineth after me,
Salvation be thy leading Staff,
To set the Sinner free....
Now Glory be to God on High,

> Salvation high and low;
> And thus the Soul on Christ rely,
> To Heaven surely go.
> Come, Blessed Jesus, Heavenly Dove,
> Accept Repentance here;
> Salvation give, with tender Love;
> Let us with Angels share.

Within a generation, black Christian leaders had become the most effective preachers to blacks, both slave and non-slave. David George was converted in 1770 under the preaching of a fellow slave; almost immediately he began to preach himself. By the outbreak of the American War of Independence, George had helped found a black Baptist church in Silver Bluff, South Carolina. He then was liberated by the British who offered freedom to slaves who supported their cause in the American Revolution. With other freed slaves he was transported by the British to Nova Scotia, where he helped start Canada's first black churches. A few years later George joined the immigration of blacks from Nova Scotia to Sierra Leone. In that West African colony, which philanthropists in the William Wilberforce circle were opening up as a refuge for former slaves, George once again founded a Baptist church. His journey of faith began in American slavery and ended with missionary outreach in Africa. It would take some time, but the pattern of George's life eventually set the norm of African churches founded and governed by Africans.

Richard Allen was a contemporary of David George, also converted as a slave who purchased his own freedom and took the lead in forming a self-standing African American variety of Protestantism. Allen was encouraged by Methodist itinerants, including Francis Asbury who in 1794 presided at the dedication of Allen's Bethel Church in Philadelphia. Although antagonistic whites tried hard to stop the building of this church, it became a lighthouse for black Christians and the flagship of African American Methodism. Black American churches like those started by George and Allen shared much of the era's standard evangelical ethos, but they were also set apart by how the Christian faith was adapted to the powerless and by how it sustained generations of believers in the face of systemic racial prejudice. The seeds of what flowered with Martin Luther King, Jr in the civil-rights campaigns of the 1950s and 1960s were planted by these 18th-century pioneers.

A Baptist shoemaker with scant formal education was a key figure in stimulating Protestant missions from Britain and the English-speaking world more generally. William Carey was inspired as a young boy by the published diary of David Brainerd, a colonial American missionary to the Delaware Indians, and by the travel journals of Captain James Cook who transfixed Europeans with his accounts of the South Seas. When Carey's initial missionary interests were stifled by local indifference, he began intensive self-education in biblical Hebrew and Greek and in literature on conditions in the non-Christian world. Two signal events followed in 1792. First was the publication of Carey's *Enquiry into the Obligations of Christians to Use Means for the Conversion of the Heathens*, a stirring apology for cross-cultural missionary service and a wide-ranging survey of the un-evangelized populations of the globe. Second was the creation of an independent voluntary organization, the Baptist Missionary Society, to commission and support foreign workers.

The voluntary mission society was a haphazardly discovered vehicle of great future importance, not only for organizing Protestantism in the United States but also for spurring the great wave of Protestant missionary expansion in the century that followed. Christendom, which to that point had been the default option for Protestant organization, was giving way to something more free form, creative, multi-directed and harder to control.

Carey himself arrived in India in 1793 with the first small contingent of English Baptist missionaries. During the next 40 years, he overcame opposition from the East India Company that fiercely protected its mercantile connections against all potential disruption, including Christian conversion and Christian ethics. He went on to publish Bible translations in Bengali and Sanskrit and to use a printing press imported from England for publishing portions of the Bible in over forty other Indian languages. The most notable difficulty of Carey's career was the mental breakdown of his wife Dorothy who had been most reluctant to leave her native land.

In light of Dorothy Carey's difficulties, it was ironic that Carey became a major inspiration for Adoniram Judson, the pioneer of American missionary work. Judson gained renown in Protestant circles for what he did in Burma, but the most notable feature of his career may have been the contributions of Ann Hasseltine Judson (1789–1826), the bride who accompanied him to the Far East. In the words of historian Dana Robert, 'as a missionary wife in Burma, she adopted orphans, taught girls, translated Bible portions, and wrote the first history of an American mission'. Significantly, her life rather than Dorothy Carey's became the model for much later activity. After some indecision about commissioning women as full-fledged missionaries, most Western societies were doing so by the latter part of the 19th century, at which time female Protestant volunteers substantially outnumbered the men. Significantly, these women missionaries were often particularly effective in recruiting native 'Bible women' who usually remained unnamed but who were often the key agents of advance.

N. Rogers Pinx.ᵗ   Alex Cameron Sc.

7. Ann Judson died young; Adoniram Judson lived a long life; both had a great influence in encouraging Protestant missionary efforts

A final important factor in the first blossoming of Protestant missionary effort was the leadership of several far-sighted mission executives. Henry Venn of the Anglican Church Missionary Society encouraged missionaries to establish churches that would be self-governing, self-supporting, and self-propagating. He also

C. Harding Pinx.ᵗ   Alex Cameron Eng.ʳ

7. Continued

spoke provocatively about the 'euthanasia of the mission' as a constant goal for missionary service; they were to die so that new churches might live. Other influential leaders who supported similar goals were Rufus Anderson of the American Board of Commissioners for Foreign Missions and John Nevius, an American Presbyterian missionary to China and Korea.

China

In China, where a Catholic presence had existed since missions by the Jesuits in the 16th century, the first Protestant did not arrive until the early 19th century. That missionary, Robert Morrison, was thoroughly dedicated to his goals of translating the New Testament into Chinese, preparing Chinese grammars and dictionaries, and converting native Chinese to Christianity. Through exhaustive labours, he succeeded in the first two goals but only minimally in the third. Morrison's work was both facilitated and hampered by his connections with Britain's East India Company. The company gave him employment as a translator, but its increasing involvement in the opium trade forced the missionary to countenance what he, and later Chinese opinion, detested as the worst kind of callous imperialism.

Particularly after the Opium Wars of the 1840s opened Chinese ports to Western trade, Protestant interest in Chinese missions grew very rapidly. Until the Communist Revolution after the Second World War, more Western Protestant missionaries would be active in China than in any other single location. Much of that often very sacrificial missionary effort was aimed at seeing Chinese churches, schools, and hospitals develop in imitation of Western models. Yet China also enjoyed a consistent line of missionaries who may have shared those goals, but who also intimated the possibility of Chinese churches more fully adapted to Chinese culture. Karl Gutzlaff, whom Robert Morrison helped recruit, founded the Chinese Union in 1844 with the goal of enlisting Chinese Christians as key agents of Chinese evangelism, but this work floundered due to Gutzlaff's own over-enthusiasm and the unreliability of his first recruits. Hudson Taylor, who founded the China Inland Mission in 1865, was much more successful in recruiting Western missionaries and at encouraging them to learn Chinese, enlist Chinese partners in the work, and adapt as far as possible to Chinese conditions.

Landmarks on the way to indigenized churches included one of the most tragic civil conflicts in Chinese history. The Taiping Rebellion of 1850 to 1864 was led by Hong Xiuquan whose Heavenly Kingdom reflected at least some influence from a Protestant tract and some exposure to biblical stories. Neither Hong's movement nor the civil strife it occasioned can be called Protestant, but it did represent an early instance of Western Christian concepts seasoning a Chinese utopian vision, and with startling results.

Much more thoroughly Protestant were the labours of Pastor Xi (or Hsi) Shengmo, a convert of Taylor's China Inland Mission who became known as Xi the Overcomer of Demons. Xi was active in the northern province of Shanxi where he became a much respected local preacher after a terrible period of famine and after he set up as many as fifty centres for opium addicts where he distributed his own 'Life-establishing Pills' as an antidote to addiction. Xi, who died in 1896 as the troubles of the Qing dynasty were coming to a climax, avidly studied the Scripture, practised physical and spiritual healing, engaged in spiritual warfare, and was the recipient of special communications from God. In each of these, he filled the forms of traditional Chinese culture with new content defined by the Holiness emphases so prominent in the China Inland Mission.

After 1900, when 'the League of Righteous Fists' (the Boxers) lashed out at all foreigners, including missionaries, and especially at Chinese Christian converts, even more Chinese-directed Christian movements emerged. They reflected in peaceful ways the same desire to escape Western influence that the Boxers expressed violently. The enterprising Dora Yu (Yu Cidu) worked with Western missionaries in Shanghai and also for a short while in Korea before she struck off in 1910 with her own summer Bible classes and eventually the Jiangwan Bible School. For many decades, the activities of Chinese believers like Dora Yu would be overshadowed by individuals and organizations more closely allied with missionary efforts. But they were the ones who laid the foundations for Chinese-directed, Protestant-like churches that would be able to survive when the harsh persecutions of the Chinese communist regime began.

Africa

A similar account for Africa also acknowledges the importance of Western pioneering efforts but again recognizes that Protestant Christianity took firm root in Africa only when Africans did the planting, watering, cultivating, and harvesting. Thus, for Africa's modern Christian history, Thomas Fowell Buxton is an important figure for trying to end the slave trade by bringing 'Christianity, Commerce, and Civilization' to the Niger River Valley with a famous Expedition in 1841. The even more famous Dr. David Livingstone is even more important for his tireless efforts in the Zambezi River region during the mid-century decades at educating, evangelizing, and healing Africans still beset by the ravages of the slave trade. The well-intended efforts of Buxton, Livingstone, and a few more of their peers would be greatly complicated by the imperial onslaught that rolled out of Europe from the 1880s to the 1950s.

But for African Christianity, Western forces were never as important as what key African figures like Samuel Ajayi Crowther accomplished. As a youth Crowther was captured by African slave traders and in 1822 dispatched for a life of bondage in the Americas when he was rescued by a British naval squadron and set ashore at Freetown, Sierra Leone. In this colony designed by British philanthropists as a haven for liberated slaves, Crowther was educated, converted, and soon drawn into contact with missionaries of Henry Venn's Church Missionary Society. Crowther then led a successful missionary band to his native Yorubaland where they were able to establish flourishing churches. So impressive was Crowther in these tasks and as a gifted linguist that Venn saw to Crowther's ordination first as an

8. Samuel Ajayi Crowther was the first African Anglican bishop

Anglican minister and then, in 1864, as a missionary bishop of the
Church of England – the first non-European in such a post.
Crowther was given the impossible task of overseeing pioneering
work in the far reaches of the Niger Valley where few Europeans
had yet ventured and where Islam and African primal faiths
shared the allegiance of the people. Yet he proved an effective
preacher, he had much success in translating the Scriptures into
African languages, and he was one of his era's most effective
Christian communicators with Muslims (with patient

comparisons between the Bible and the Qur'an as the key). Toward the end of his life, he was criticized and then shunted aside by a new generation of English missionaries who questioned the shape of his spirituality and his control of African assistants. As a result of the rising imperial tide, there were far fewer initiatives transferring power to African church leaders. Only after the Second World War and the continent-wide movement to African independence would it be clear how important Crowther's work had been. He was a father in God indeed for the extraordinary growth of Protestant-like churches in Africa that has taken place since the coming of independence.

Chapter 6
Pentecostals, revival, independents

During the early 20th century, Protestantism entered a new stage of worldwide development. Outside of Europe and North America, missionary initiatives sometimes led to churches that resembled what the missionaries knew in their homelands. Almost as often they resulted in new movements that found the traditions of Western Christianity partially or entirely irrelevant. These movements developed in myriad different ways – often in connection with periods of revival – but together they constituted a new independent sphere of Protestant and Protestant-like churches. Reinforcing and even precipitating the emergence of independent movements was Pentecostalism, which burst onto the world with startling effect. Together independency and Pentecostalism carried the story of international Protestantism into uncharted territory.

Pentecostalism in the United States

A once-standard picture depicted the rise of Pentecostalism as an American event. This picture is not entirely amiss, even if broader attention to Africa, Asia, and Latin America has shown that important features of the American story were being replicated in other parts of the world at about the same time.

In the United States, modern Pentecostalism appeared in the first decade of the 20th century when several earlier strands of Protestant piety flowed together. One strand was the Holiness teaching that originated with John Wesley and that emphasized 'the baptism of the Holy Spirit' as a more advanced stage of spiritual development after conversion. In 19th-century Britain, a parallel emphasis on 'full surrender' to the Holy Spirit had been featured during annual summer meetings at Keswick in England's Lake District. Belief in the possibility of divine physical healing was also widespread among many Protestants, both elites and common people, during the last decades of the 19th century. African American and Hispanic Protestants practised a more expressive and emotional faith that also contributed to the new movement.

When these strands came together under the effective preaching of leaders like Charles Parham, a Holiness advocate of entire sanctification, and William Seymour, a mild-mannered African American who taught listeners to expect the baptism of the Holy Ghost, spiritual experiences of escalating intensity were the result. These experiences culminated in a great revival beginning in 1906 at the Apostolic Faith Gospel Mission on Azusa Street in Los Angeles. In this revival, participants experienced the Holy Spirit's unmediated power in divine healing, visions, words of prophecy, and especially the gift of tongues as evidence of the Spirit's in-dwelling presence.

News of events at Azusa Street spread rapidly, drawing visitors from Chicago, New York, and the upper South who returned to their homes with new experiences and the new Pentecostal teaching. Before long, visitors from overseas were making the same pilgrimage with the same results. Soon American Pentecostal missionaries were themselves going overseas with the message of baptism in the Holy Spirit, and the revival spread farther and faster.

'Pentecostals' and 'charismatics'

Early Pentecostals often proclaimed a four-fold message depicting Christ as Saviour, Baptizer (or Sanctifier), Healer, and Coming King. Along with emphasizing standard Christian teaching on salvation in Christ, Pentecostals also joined many other Protestants, especially of a more evangelical type, in stressing the near-return of Christ and in expecting physical healing as a divine gift.

The most distinctive Pentecostal teaching concerns speaking in tongues, which is viewed as a sign-gift from the Holy Spirit marking the sanctification of believers. Speaking in tongues is a practice based on New Testament passages like Acts 2:4, where listeners at Pentecost heard the disciples of Jesus speaking in their own languages. It also draws on the Apostle Paul's account in the First Epistle to the Corinthians about 'speaking in a tongue', which referred to a kind of ecstatic spiritual speech. For almost all Pentecostals, speaking in tongues remains a definite sign of the baptism of the Holy Spirit, although modern tongues-speaking is usually ecstatic utterance rather than the miraculous gift of communicating in other languages.

From the 1960s, charismatic movements of several types spread rapidly around the globe. Charismatic gifts resemble what has been experienced among Pentecostals, but charismatics usually do not form separate denominations defined by these experiences. Instead, they are often identified as 'charismatic Anglicans', 'charismatic independents', 'charismatic Catholics', and the like.

In a United States that still took racial separation for granted, Azusa Street was also remarkable for the way that blacks and Hispanics joined whites in the nightly meetings. After the early halcyon period, however, long-standing differences reappeared, with blacks and whites organizing themselves into separate

Pentecostal denominations. In 1914, the Assemblies of God emerged from several networks of periodicals and faith-healing circuits as the most important Pentecostal denomination among Caucasians. The largest black Pentecostal denomination was the Church of God in Christ, which had earlier been organized as a Holiness body. After its key early leader, Charles H. Mason (1866–1961), journeyed to Azusa Street, the part of the denomination that became Pentecostal rapidly expanded in the United States and to many places overseas.

In general, however, denominational concerns were not priorities in those early years. Later observers noted that Pentecostalism spread most rapidly among self-disciplined, often mobile folk of the middle and lower-middle classes. But a still more common characteristic was ardent desire for the unmediated experience of the Holy Spirit.

Pentecostalism worldwide

A global perspective on Pentecostalism does not deny the importance of Azusa Street. Events in the United States did, in fact, often provide the impetus for parallel movements around the world. But as suggested recently by the Nigerian historian Ogbu Kalu, the world's incredibly diverse range of Pentecostal movements has been fed by many streams. Local appropriation of the Bible, local religious practices, and local conceptions of spiritual warfare between good and evil spirits created worldviews primed for Pentecostalism long before the explicit Pentecostal message arrived. Others have also joined Kalu in his observation that Pentecostal-type Christianity was ready to take off in conditions stimulated by the accelerating pace of economic globalization: 'oases of wealth in the desert of scorching poverty, class conflicts, legitimacy crises, and ... stunted populations'. In such conditions, the Pentecostal insistence on the immediate presence of a loving God and the immediate work of an all-powerful Holy Spirit create a Christian faith with gripping appeal. The American experience remains important as a model, less so as a genealogical ancestor.

The extent of that appeal is underscored by the enumerators who put together the recently published *Atlas of Global Christianity*. They count over 600 million 'renewalists', or one out of ten people on the planet, as members of Pentecostal denominations or Christian adherents strongly identified by Pentecostal or charismatic characteristics.

The several flourishing Pentecostal denominations in Chile exemplify a common pattern by which Pentecostal movements come into existence. All of them originated from the work of Willis Collins Hoover, a Methodist Holiness missionary from the United States who had first come to Chile in 1889. Events at Azusa Street intrigued Hoover, but even more important were earlier reports from India and elsewhere about unusual responses to the presence of the Holy Spirit. When Pentecostal phenomena broke out in Hoover's Valparaiso Methodist church, it led to a division between Methodists and Pentecostals, but also to rapid Pentecostal advance. As has been said by several observers, the spark for Pentecostal renewal may have come from outside Chile, but the material bursting into flames was home-grown.

Wales and Korea

It remains noteworthy that Pentecostal-like revival broke out in many different places during the first decade of the 20th century. In Wales, the excitement that lasted through much of 1904 and 1905 was mostly contained within Welsh dissenting Protestant churches. Yet the long meetings, the fervent singing, the willingness to confess sins publicly, the prominence of lay leaders all represented elements that would soon characterize Pentecostal movements elsewhere in the world. The great publicity generated by the revival reverberated around the globe, as in this report from a Londoner who visited Wales in late 1904:

And all this vast quivering, throbbing, singing, praying, exultant multitude intensely conscious of the all-pervading influence of some invisible reality…called it the Spirit of God. Those who have not witnessed it may call it what they will; I am inclined to agree with those on the spot.

In Korea, similar events with even longer-lasting effects occurred at about the same time. Protestants of any kind were scarce in the early 20th century, but already the movement had gained some of the traction that would make Korea's Presbyterian, Pentecostal, and Methodist churches among the world's most vibrant in the century that followed. From the start, missionaries from the United States and Canada made a point of handing over responsibility for church leadership as soon as possible. The Bible translation that missionaries and Koreans cooperated to publish was not in the elite Korean language tied closely to Chinese but in *Hangul*, or people's Korean, which made it an almost instant bestseller. Also important was the fact that Christianity functioned as a liberating, anti-imperial force. Unlike much of the rest of the modern world, where Christianity came along with the colonizers, Christianity in Korea offered support for a people who suffered first under Chinese dominance and then from Japan's harsh colonial regime.

The events that brought world attention to Korea were revivals that began at Pyongyang early in the century and climaxed during an intense season of renewal in 1907. At a training session organized by the Presbyterians in January of that year, Koreans and missionaries publicly confessed their sins, experienced what was described as 'a rush of power from without [that] seemed to take hold of the meeting', and prayed out loud together (thus beginning the distinctively Korean practice of simultaneous group prayer). Similar meetings that strengthened the new Protestant communities throughout Korea soon spread from Pyongyang.

In both Wales and Korea, the nearly simultaneous revivals eventually led to the formation of Pentecostal churches and other new denominations. The great difference between the two was that in Wales revival enthusiasm eventually cooled, and the principality followed the general European pattern of secular de-Christianization. By contrast, in Korea the revival energies never flagged. Less than a century after Protestant missionaries had come to Korea, Korean churches were dispatching their own missionaries to many other places in the world.

India

In India, the story was slightly different as the newer Pentecostal tide merged with singularly Indian features to create the current situation with a full range of Indian Protestant churches, some in communion with Western denominations, but others resolutely independent. The way in which revival and independency have coexisted is well illustrated in the extraordinary career of Pandita Ramabai whose parents broke with custom by giving their daughter a thorough education in Sanskrit and the Hindu sacred texts. After her parents and one sister died of starvation in 1874, Ramabai continued her studies and eventually won local renown as 'the Pandita', or teacher, of Indian religious works. Even after her marriage in 1880, she continued her campaign for women's rights and against the ancestral practice of child marriage. When her husband died shortly thereafter, Ramabai was left with an infant daughter and a very insecure future. She had earlier been introduced to Christianity, but had not been impressed until she enjoyed fruitful conversations with an English Baptist missionary, Isaac Allen, and then met missionary representatives of the Anglican Community of St Mary the Virgin. Eventually, the Anglican sisters sponsored her travel to England where in September 1883 she professed Christian faith. Ramabai returned to India via the United States where she delivered well-attended lectures that were published as *The High-Caste Hindu Woman*, a book that catalogued abuses and appealed for reform on Christian principles. Back in India in 1889, she opened Sharada Sadan ('home of learning') in Bombay/Mumbai, a school and home for

9. Pandita Ramabai is shown here at work on her translation of the Bible into Marathi

high-caste child widows. Soon she set up a more extensive operation in the nearby city of Pune that came to include a home for mistreated and homeless child widows, a home for boys, an asylum for prostitutes, a workshop for the blind, and a home for the aged. These institutions also collected resources that Ramabai used to relieve local famines. In 1898, she founded an explicitly Christian work in Kedgaon, near Pune, entitled the Mukti Mission.

In 1905, a revival with many Pentecostal signs occurred at this mission, which has remained independent throughout its continuing existence. There was fervent prayer, physical healings, speaking in tongues, and the exorcism of demons. In the wake of this unusual spiritual outpouring, Ramabai intensified her explicitly Christian work, which included translating the Scriptures into Marathi. In her own conception of the Christian faith, the kindly treatment that Jesus accorded to the Samaritan woman, as recorded in the fourth chapter of John's gospel, remained central. She represented an early expression of Indian Protestantism more closely tied to Indian conditions than to Western Christian traditions of any sort.

Africa

The most extensive growth of independent and Pentecostal-type Protestantism has taken place in sub-Saharan Africa where the synergy of supernatural Christianity and African primal religions has produced a stunning array of new Christian movements. Signs of things to come were visible very early on. When the British were just beginning their move into South Africa, they encountered not only the well-established Dutch settlements, but also Africans keenly interested in Christianity. One of them was Ntsikana, the son of a Xhosa chief. After a vision in 1815, Ntsikana taught his followers to observe Sunday as a day of rest, to receive baptism, and to pray to the one true God. Although Ntsikana sustained some contact with British and Dutch missionaries, his faith owed little directly to their ministrations. He became an effective evangelist, a respected teacher, an advocate of pacifism, and the author of hymns that are still sung in South African churches.

Ntsikana hymn

Of Ntsikana's four hymns, the 'great hymn' still appears in many South African hymnals:

> The Great God, He is in heaven.
> Thou art thou, Shield of truth.
> Thou art thou, Stronghold of truth.
> Thou art thou, Thicket of truth.
> Thou art thou, who dwellest in the highest.
> Who created life (below) and created (life) above.
> The Creator who created, created heaven.
> This maker of the stars, and the Pleiades.
> A star flashed forth, telling us
> The maker of the blind, does
> He not make them on purpose?

The trumpet sounded, it has called us,
As for His hunting, He hunteth for souls.
Who draweth together flocks opposed to each other.
The Leader, he led us.
Whose great mantle, we put it on.
Those hands of Thine, they are wounded
Those feet of Thine, they are wounded.
Thy blood, why is it streaming?
Thy blood, it was shed for us.
This great price, have we called for it?
This home of Thine, have we called for it?

The move toward African independent churches became stronger towards the end of the 19th century. It was a function of increased missionary success among Africans combined with increased African resentment of colonialism. Garrick Braide illustrated what became a relatively common process. He was a protégé of James 'Holy' Johnson, the second black African Anglican bishop who followed Samuel Ajayi Crowther in being asked to oversee Anglican efforts in the Niger Delta. Johnson, who was more willing than Crowther to incorporate elements of African traditional religion, had also been influenced by the Africanist ideology of Edward Blyden from Liberia that compared Islam favourably to Christianity. Braide was one of Bishop Johnson's most effective catechists, but he soon developed a separate following because of his healing and prophetic gifts. The Christian faith that Braide proclaimed included many elements of strict evangelical practice. He attacked alcohol abuse, called for Sunday rest, urged converts to destroy their fetishes, and warned them against the evils of warfare. When during the First World War he expressed the opinion that the age of the black man was soon going to replace the age of the white man, he was slapped in prison by the British for sedition. By that time, however, an independent Christ Army Church of perhaps a million strong had broken away from the

Anglicans in order to follow the one they called 'Elijah II'. After Braide's death in 1918, most of his followers sustained their independence, but in a multitude of churches that splintered from the Church Army in Nigeria and surrounding countries.

The process by which Western Protestant beginnings has lead on to indigenous African churches is well illustrated by the story of William Wadé Harris. In 1910, Harris was put in a Liberian prison for supporting attempts at replacing the African American government of that country with a regime under British influence. Harris had been raised as a Methodist, but then worked for many years with Episcopalians as a catechist and teacher. While in prison, Harris was visited by the Angel Gabriel in what Harris later described alternatively as a vision and a palpable revelation. The angel addressed Harris as a prophet of the last times, told him to set aside Western dress in favour of a white robe, and commanded him to destroy the fetishes that were a part of the region's traditional African religions. The angel also said that Harris was to immediately baptize all who would receive this Christian sacrament rather than follow the missionary practice of requiring converts to undergo a long period of instruction. This last message was crucial: missionary conversions had been scarce because their caution left new Christians spiritually unprotected between the time of giving up the old religion and the time of full incorporation into the new. Harris's programme removed that fear at a stroke.

After Harris was released from prison, he began to preach this new message in the nearby Ivory Coast. The impact in July 1913 was dramatic. Listeners were impressed by the fervor of Harris' Christ-centred message, but also by its power. Harris won an immediate reputation as a healer. Additional stories circulated of colonial administrators who died unexpectedly after they interfered with Harris, and likewise of sudden death coming upon those who were baptized after claiming to have destroyed their fetishes, but who had only buried them. Thousands flocked to hear Harris and then to organize locally around the twelve apostles he regularly

10. The prophet William Wadé Harris was especially effective at communicating a Christian message in West Africa at the start of the 20th century

appointed in converted communities. When Harris urged converts to connect with missionary churches, the small Catholic and Protestant congregations in the Ivory Coast, the Gold Coast (Ghana), and surrounding regions were overwhelmed. Some converts who never found a home with the missionaries created their own autonomous Harrist church, which remains a major presence in the region. Missionaries, who objected to Harris' toleration of polygamy, nonetheless benefited greatly from his work.

Many other African Initiated (or Independent) Churches have followed the Harris pattern, with the Church of Jesus Christ on Earth by the Prophet Simon Kimbangu among the best known. This church began with a public ministry of healing, preaching, and teaching by Simon Kimbangu in the Belgian Congo in the years immediately after the First World War. Despite the Belgians harsh reprisals that included imprisoning Kimbangu from 1921 until his death thirty years later, the movement endured. When the Kimbanguist church finally received official recognition in the late 1950s, shortly before the end of Belgian rule, it was a million strong. In 1970, the Church of Jesus Christ on Earth by the Prophet Simon Kimbangu was the first African Independent Church to become a member of the World Council of Churches. By 1995, it numbered between seven and eight million members.

The Harrist and Kimbanguist churches have taken their place in a full array of independent churches that have spread across Africa over the last century of dramatic Christianization. Martinus Daneel, a Zimbabwean and life-long participant-observer of these churches, has classified them in the following general scheme: Ethiopian (which draw upon Psalm 68:1 – 'Ethiopia shall soon stretch out her hands unto God' – to create independent, usually non-prophetic churches that remain close to missionary roots); *Spirit-Type* (which emphasize prophesying, healing, speaking in tongues, and other Pentecostal phenomena and that are known as Zionist or Apostolic in South Africa, and Aladura in West Africa); *Prophet-Healer* (which regard a central figure as honoured prophet or even Christ-like figure, including the Kimbanguists as well as Johane Maranke's African Apostolic Church in Zimbabwe and Isaac Shembe's Nazerite Baptist Church among the Zulus); and *Neo-Pentecostal* (which describes newer groups that stress health-and-wealth in their preaching and often have closer ties to Western Pentecostal or charismatic figures).

The range of teaching, practice, and organization within African Independent Churches is vast. If the independent churches of the Indian subcontinent, China, the South Pacific, and Latin America were added, that range would be even broader. Some of these churches promote teaching, like the deification of the founder, clearly at odds with main Christian traditions; many are entirely in line with those traditions; still others occupy a quasi-Christian zone similar to where some European Christian movements resided in the early Middle Ages. Almost all of them are marked by intense appropriation of at least some parts of the Bible, by the presence of charismatic leadership, and by liberation from Western supervision. Some have created or helped African movements for cultural, social, economic, environmental, or political development. In general, they may be regarded as the most recent extension of the adaptability, the initiative, the personal dynamism, and the biblical fixation of historical Protestantism.

Chapter 7
Whither the West?

Over the first half of the 20th century, while Protestantism in many varieties was expanding rapidly in the non-Western world and American Protestantism developed from a regional into an international force, European Protestants suffered a number of reversals. At the start of the century, it was still taken for granted that the goals, energy, leaders, programmes, and aspirations of Protestants in Europe and North America defined world Protestantism, and that Protestants still possessed real authority for substantial parts of life in substantial regions of their historical homelands. As the century wore on, both assumptions were challenged, partly because of developments within the Protestant churches but mostly because of the overwhelming force of world events.

Edinburgh 1910

The World Missionary Conference that convened in Edinburgh at the Assembly Hall of the United Free Church of Scotland in June 1910 was a landmark in Protestant missionary history. The 1,200 delegates who attended included a substantial number from continental Europe and a few from outside the West, but the great majority came from Britain and North America. Many who addressed the gathering expressed the hope that the kind of Christian cooperation witnessed on mission fields would catch fire in Protestant homelands as well. Besides the theme of Christian unity, the conference also directed major attention to evangelization in the non-Christian world, the churches' support of education, the relationship of churches to governments, and the encounter between Christianity and non-Christian religions. As a reflection of ambiguity toward Roman Catholicism, the conference had no delegates from Latin America and generally avoided talking about that part of the 'Christian' but 'not Protestant' world. The general expectation was that strategizing at Edinburgh and similar Western gatherings would continue to direct the course of world Protestantism for a very long time to come.

At the event, a different future unfolded. The conference marked a transition from Protestantism defined as a Western faith to a

11. The Edinburgh Missionary Conference of 1910 was the largest gathering of Protestant missionary personnel to that time

situation where Protestants in North America and Europe would exist alongside a profusion of local movements scattered around the world. The few minority voices who did address the meeting were prescient. Vedanayagam Samuel Azariah came from India where, besides working closely with the YMCA and Anglican bishops dispatched from Britain, he had also helped establish several self-standing Indian missionary agencies. Shortly after the conference ended he would be named the first Indian bishop for the Anglican church in South Asia. At Edinburgh, he offered a gentle protest against Western patronizing: 'Through all the ages to come the Indian Church will rise up in gratitude to attest the heroism and self-denying labours of the missionary body. You have given your goods to feed the poor. You have given your bodies to be burned.' But then he went on to ask for yet a higher gift: 'We ask also for *love*. Give us FRIENDS!'

It is evident in retrospect that Azariah spoke as much for the future as did the delegates who assumed ongoing Western dominance. Yet if Europeans and Americans were no longer to control the coming decades, Edinburgh did leave a powerful legacy with far-reaching effects. Discussions and personal connections begun at Edinburgh eventually led to the founding of the International Missionary Council (1921) and then less directly to two other significant organizations. The Universal Christian Conference on Life and Work met for the first time at Stockholm in 1925; it explored ways in which Protestant churches might cooperate on practical social questions. The World Conference on Faith and Order held its inaugural meeting at Lausanne in 1927; it pursued consideration of doctrine and practice more directly. In turn, these two organizations provided the main constituents that in 1948 combined to create the World Council of Churches.

Related ecumenical currents also contributed to church mergers in various parts of the world. Among the most notable of these was the formation of the Church of South India in 1947 and the

Church of North India in 1970, both of which united Anglicans with a number of other Protestant bodies. While the World Council of Churches and related ecumenical organizations never spoke for many evangelical, Pentecostal, fundamentalist, and sectarian Protestants, its programmes and international meetings went on to provide unprecedented opportunities for dialogue and cooperation among the older, more traditional denominations and many non-Western Protestants linked to these same groups.

A movement parallel to the Edinburgh venture that also illustrated the reach (and limits) of international Protestantism was the wide network of church leaders that promoted world peace in general and the League of Nations in particular. The network was a thoroughly Protestant enterprise that combined a general reliance on biblical principles with specific commitment to the ideals of Western democracy. It was led before, during, and after the First World War by reform-minded internationalists who worked tirelessly to improve contacts among churches and promote global peace-keeping organizations. Key leaders included the Canadian-born English manufacturer and long-time member of the British Parliament, Joseph Baker, who brought his Quaker convictions to this task; William Howard Taft, president of the United States from 1909 to 1913 and a Unitarian whose faith played a part in his efforts for the American League to Enforce Peace and then for the League of Nations; and Friedrich Siegmund-Schultze, a theologian headquartered in Berlin whose international Protestant connections sustained his opposition to German militarism. These efforts were important in many spheres, not least for enlisting a large circle of international allies to campaign for both world Protestant cooperation and the League of Nations. It came to include Jan Christiaan Smuts, the South African general and statesman for whom a modified version of the Dutch Reformed faith of his youth guided him throughout life, and Nitobe Inazo, the Japanese civil servant and diplomat who combined Quaker faith and a discriminating promotion of ancestral Japanese ideals.

Although these international Protestants were ultimately as disappointed in what the League of Nations accomplished as delegates to Edinburgh were in what the West could do for world Christianity, these intersecting networks of reformers represented Protestant international aspirations at their best.

War and theology in Europe

The death and destruction of the First World War (1914–18) brought the idealism of Western Protestants down to earth. Critics of Christendom have accurately charged that when institutional Christianity dominated Europe, it had often led to inhumane disaster. But nothing in Christendom's long, admittedly fallible history could match the violence that engulfed Europe as the 20th century unfolded. In the First World War, alternatives for traditional faith that had strengthened over the previous century combined with malignant effect. Competing nationalisms, scientific technology (which produced poison gas, machine gun, barbed wire, tank, and bomber), and propaganda unleashed through the marvels of mass communication all joined forces to slaughter a generation of European young men and lay waste a continent. When Protestants lent enthusiastic support to the war effort, as many did in Britain and Germany, the result in the climate of post-war reaction was loss of credibility for the churches.

For any who still considered Europe the centre of 'Christian civilization', the First World War spelled disillusionment. The families of the dead, wounded, and traumatized suffered a severe test of faith. In the wake of the war, much of Europe and North America turned rapidly away from God to pursue pleasure: in the United States it became 'the roaring twenties', in Berlin the promotion of blatant public decadence. The chaos of politics, economies, and ideologies that followed the end of the First World War, the even greater death and destruction of the Second World War, the division of Europe into West-bloc and East-bloc that followed the defeat of Nazism, the sudden collapse of Marxist regimes and the tangled course of reconstruction in the wake of this collapse all severely strained the efforts of churches to manage, or even fathom, events. Especially troubling was the problem of theodicy created by the genocidal assault of Nazi Germany on European Jews. Theodicy is the question of how to continue believing in a benevolent God when confronted by destructive evils of the worst kind. Convincing answers were hard to come by, even as the faithful witness of believers under great pressure did testify to the enduring power of the Christian gospel.

It was certainly not the case that Protestant theologians were struck dumb by the ravages of war, although many convictions once widely accepted did ring hollow. Adolf von Harnack's sanguine picture of divine fatherhood and human brotherhood and the depiction by Ernst Troeltsch of God as an imminent force flowing with human history seemed inadequate for the crises of the hour.

The trauma of war hastened the arrival of theological alternatives. In 1929, the Swiss theologian Emil Brunner published *The Theology of Crisis*, a book that criticized theology governed by humanistic or anthropomorphic assumptions. Brunner's title provided the name for a diverse group of theologians who joined in criticizing complacent assumptions about human progress, but whose positive solutions moved in several different directions. It was also called 'dialectical theology' (for positing sharp contradictions between God and humanity) and 'neo-orthodoxy' (for retrieving some elements of classical Reformation teachings).

In the early years of the Third Reich, as the Nazis solidified their hold on Germany and enlisted a number of Protestants as their supporters, other church leaders promulgated the Barmen Declaration (1934) that spoke out courageously against the 'German Christianity' adapting itself to Hitlerism. During the Second World War itself, the young Lutheran pastor Dietrich Bonhoeffer boldly attacked 'cheap grace' and called nominal believers back to the integrity of Christ. His own life became a memorial to this appeal

12. Dietrich Bonhoeffer (centre) is shown here with Italian cellmates not long before he was executed

when, for assisting a plot to assassinate Hitler, he was executed by the Nazis in the last days of the European war. The Anglican bishop, George Bell, displayed a different kind of courage in chastising the Allies for indiscriminate fire bombing of German cities. The French pastor, André Trocmé, drew on the traditions of his historic Reformed faith to motivate the rescue of Jewish children. And in the immediate post-war years, Helmuth Thielicke from his pulpit in bombed-out Hamburg powerfully proclaimed a message of gospel hope given shape by a revived theology of the Reformation.

The most important theological voice of the era, and probably the most significant Protestant theologian since Friedrich Schleiermacher, was Karl Barth (1886–1968). Barth received a conventional theological education that featured progressive optimism about the human condition and the civilized gentility of

Barmen Declaration

From the Barmen Declaration (1934):

> In view of the errors of the 'German Christians' and of the present Reich Church Administration, which are ravaging the Church and at the same time also shattering the unity of the German Evangelical Church, we confess the following evangelical truths:
>
> 1. 'I am the way, and the truth, and the life: no one comes to the Father, but by me.' (John 14:6) 'Truly, truly, I say to you, he who does not enter the sheepfold by the door but climbs in by another way, that man is a thief and a robber.... I am the door; if anyone enters by me, he will be saved.' (John 10:1, 9).
>
> Jesus Christ, as he is attested to us in Holy Scripture, is the one Word of God whom we have to hear, and whom we have to trust and obey in life and in death.
>
> We reject the false doctrine that the Church could and should recognize as a source of its proclamation, beyond and besides this one Word of God, yet other events, powers, historic figures and truths as God's revelation.

God. He was shaken from these views by the carnage of the First World War, but even more by the realization that his theological training did not give him anything consequential to say to the parishioners in the little Swiss town of Safenwil where he ministered for a decade surrounding the war. The result from going back to a fresh encounter with the Scriptures and then from sympathetic attention to classics of Reformed theology was a landmark biblical commentary on the Epistle to the Romans published in 1919. Barth then became a theology professor at several German universities, during which time he played a major role in crafting the Barmen Declaration. After he was expelled from Germany in 1935, he settled in his native Switzerland, where he taught and wrote until slowed by illness a few years before his death. The fourteen volumes of his *Church Dogmatics* and many occasional writings have provided grist for ongoing theological controversy, but the main direction of his thought is clear. He wanted to see theology defined by the reality of God understood as a dynamic Trinity of love and by the gracious acts of God toward humanity that are all exemplified in the person and work of Christ.

Union and division in North America

In North America, Protestant communions adjusted slightly better to modern traumas than those in Europe. Canada, to be sure, experienced a history that eventually conformed to the European pattern. Into the 1960s, however, church attendance and other marks of religious practice remained considerably higher than in the United States. But after that time religious observance declined to levels that, while remaining above the European average, fell considerably below the American. In the years immediately after the Second World War, Canadians were leaders at the United Nations and other international gatherings in defending references to God and religious belief as critical for international peace. And when the British Parliament patriated the Canadian Constitution in 1982, an action that acknowledged full Canadian control over every aspect of Canadian government, that Constitution began with an assertion that 'Canada is founded upon principles that recognize the supremacy of God and the rule of law'. Despite these indications of hereditary religious conviction, Canada since the 1960s has secularized more comprehensively than its neighbour to the south.

Canada was one of the countries where Protestant ecumenicity enjoyed its greatest 20th-century successes. In 1925, the United Church of Canada came into being as the union of the country's Methodist, Congregational, and a majority of its Presbyterian churches. (In a roughly similar development for another member of the British Commonwealth, the Uniting Church in Australia, which was formed in 1977, joined together Methodists, Presbyterians, and Congregationalists.) In its early years, the United Church of Canada combined evangelical and social gospel emphases; subsequently, it became a champion of liberal theology and liberal social policy. After boom years following the Second World War, the United Church has suffered significant losses in the standard European pattern. While Pentecostal and a variety of evangelical churches have emerged as stronger forces in religious life, they have not replicated the dominant place that the Anglicans, Methodists, and Presbyterians once enjoyed.

Ecumenism in the United States also secured significant gains over the same period. In 1950, the National Council of Churches of Christ was founded as a successor to a Federal Council of Churches that had been launched early in the century. Through its social services arm, the Church World Service, the National Council has promoted development projects in many parts of the world. At home it was the primary sponsor of the Revised Standard Version, a major updating of the King James Bible that has enjoyed wide currency in mainline churches.

Yet divisive strife as much as unifying tranquility has marked the 20th-century history of American Protestantism. At the start of the century, a bitter controversy between modernists and fundamentalists generated immense publicity and contributed to the perception of a stark two-party division among American churches. Most critical were questions about how traditional Christian teachings should be modified in light of modern learning and moral sensibilities. Modernists wanted to treat the Scriptures as spiritual, but not particularly historical; they tended to regard the Bible's miracle stories like the virgin birth of Christ as myths communicating only religious truth; and they expressed confidence that the insights in all the world's religions would lead earnest seekers to God. Fundamentalists, by contrast, insisted on the factual reality of these and other traditional teachings. Extreme positions – Scripture as only myth vs. every part of Scripture as strictly literal, Christ's gift of salvation coming from his good example vs. Christ's significance found only in his death for sinners – were often the result. The loud voices on the theological fringes made it difficult to see that vast numbers of American Protestant adherents remained broadly traditional in what they believed, even as they accommodated themselves to much that was modern in American forms of communication, commerce, and entertainment.

Landmarks in the public debate included a multivolume series of pamphlets called *The Fundamentals* that were funded by the founders of Union Oil and published from 1910 to 1915. Contributions to the series, which were designed to shore up traditional teaching, ranged widely in learning, subtlety, and tone. But none invoked violence in the way that later groups labeled 'fundamentalist' have sometimes done. In 1922, a popular Baptist minister in New York City, Harry Emerson Fosdick, responded to what he saw as a rising tide of theological obscurantism by preaching a sermon entitled 'Shall the Fundamentalists Win?' When the sermon was widely distributed by an associate of oil magnate John D. Rockefeller, Jr, it generated additional heat.

The way religious conflict intersected with broader political forces was illustrated in the famous Scopes Trial of 1925, which challenged a law in Tennessee prohibiting the teaching of evolution. William Jennings Bryan, three times the presidential nominee of the Democratic Party, argued against evolution. For this stance, Bryan continues to be the butt of learned ridicule. Bryan, in fact, advocated a moderate position at the trial called the 'day-age' theory that interpreted the early chapters of Genesis as allowing for great expanses of time in earth's pre-history (a position that earned him the reproach of die-hard fundamentalists). Bryan's main objection to evolution was its use of social theory as justification for hypercompetitiveness in an industrial economy. But nuances of even Bryan's preliminary sort did not restrain self-styled fundamentalists from demonizing modern science or some advocates of modern science from demonizing any who objected to any of their efforts.

In a period not known for theological subtlety, the views of Reinhold Niebuhr were an exception. From his base at Union Theological Seminary in New York, and through the tumults of Depression and the Second World War, Niebuhr provided an unusual degree of sober theological reflection to both the mainline Protestant churches and some of the nation's premier intellectuals. The key to Niebuhr's thought was his dialectical reasoning about the human situation: humanity was sinful and capable of sainthood, subject to history and social forces but also molder of history and society, egotistical but capable of living for others. In the Bible, and especially the example of Christ, Niebuhr found norms for an exercise of power that depended on powerlessness.

A generation after the Scopes Trial, descendents of the earlier fundamentalists in the northern parts of the United States regrouped and presented themselves to the public as 'evangelicals'. The National Association of Evangelicals, established in 1942, gave institutional expression to this movement as did vigorous theology and journalism by young leaders like Carl F. H. Henry. The founding of Fuller Theological Seminary in California in 1947 helped sustain these initiatives, since Fuller has gone on to become the largest theological seminary in the United States outside of the Southern Baptist Convention. In addition, one of Fuller's key early trustees was the evangelist Billy Graham who emerged after the Second World War to become American's most popular preacher.

Chapter 8
From everywhere to everywhere

Protestant history from the middle of the 20th century has become more global, diverse, multiform, and complex than ever before. That diversity arises in large part from the different ways in which congregations, voluntary societies, influential personalities, and denominations have mingled practices and beliefs rooted in Protestant history with innovative responses to contemporary circumstances.

Continuities

Much in recent Protestant history does, of course, extend past trajectories into the present. To the extent that William Chillingworth was correct, when he said in the 17th century that 'the Bible...is the religion of Protestants', then the recent past has been the most Protestant era in history. The commitment to Bible translation, pivotal since the days of Martin Luther, has expanded in the West to providing different versions for different marketing niches as well as for different theological communities. In the English-speaking world, long-standing worries about the readability of the King James Version have been overlaid by recent ideological stand-offs over translating gender-related terms, by debates over translating literally or through dynamic equivalency, and by niche marketing. The result in the United States is that the

King James Version now competes for attention with the English Standard Version, the New International Version, the New King James Version, the New Revised Standard Version, and many more – often marketed in different formats for different target audiences. The gain from this situation, which is repeated on a smaller scale for other European languages, is greater comprehension. The loss is further erosion of a central Protestant, or more generally Christian, frame of reference.

The more important story about Bible distribution concerns the world at large. As of 1900, biblical portions or the whole had been translated into about 700 languages. Now, due to assiduous labours under mostly Protestant auspices, the count has risen to over 2,500. While thousands of languages remain Scripture-less, something over 95% of the world's population can read at least some part of the Bible in a first or second language.

Lamin Sanneh, born a Muslim in Gambia but then converted to Christianity and now a professor at Yale University, has shown how translation communicates unique spiritual empowerment to those who, often for the first time, hear the message of Scripture in their mother tongues. One of Sanneh's key arguments is that while the spread of Islam has brought ever increasing numbers under the globalizing influence of Arabic, the spread of Christianity binds ever-increasing numbers to their own local languages. Ironically, although missionaries may have been very clear about what they intended when they set out to translate the Scriptures, local people have often found in their newly translated Bibles things that the missionaries did not want them to see. The much more prominent place that dreams and visions hold in world Christianity as compared to traditional Western churches illustrates what happens when newer believers read the Book of Acts for themselves. Missionary organizations dedicated to Bible translation like Wycliffe International, which was founded by American missionary W. Cameron Townsend, have now become thoroughly internationalized themselves;

Wycliffe draws volunteers and financial support from partner organizations in 47 countries.

As it has been especially noteworthy in the recent past, Bible translation often brings not just an overt spiritual message but also a subtle message about the people who read the new translation, namely the intrinsic value of their own language, history, and habits of mind. The use of the Igbo Bible in Nigeria is a typical case. The Igbo, one of Nigeria's three main ethnic divisions, had possessed a Bible in their own language since the 1910s due to the work of an Anglican agent with the Church Missionary Society. But until the 1960s, the use of this Bible was tightly controlled by the missionaries. After Nigeria gained its independence, and especially after the disruption caused by the Biafran civil war of 1967 to 1970, the *Bible Nso* (Holy Bible) came alive as a guide, comfort, and encouragement to the Igbo people. The results were not necessarily calming, since liberating the Scriptures has resulted in a cacophony of Christian voices; new sects and denominations of many kinds have flourished, with each taking its inspiration from particular interpretations of Scripture. But the fragmentation of missionary Protestantism is only a secondary story; the main event is extraordinarily rapid expansion of Christian belief and extraordinary spiritual energy among those who are reading the Scriptures for themselves.

Another trajectory that has become stronger is the expanded public leadership of women in Protestant churches. In the 19th century, marginalized sectarian groups had often taken the initiative; as an example, the Quaker convictions of Susan B. Anthony grounded this American's campaigns for women's suffrage and women's rights. In other sectarian traditions like the Holiness denominations, minority Wesleyan groups, and eventually also Pentecostals, women were particularly active in preaching, evangelizing, and organizing church programmes.

For almost all Protestants, missionary service was the one domain where restrictions on female activity did not apply. The long roster of notable pioneers includes several members of the American Scudder family who preached and practised medicine in India. Mary Slessor's story illustrates the influence that one such person could exert. After her youth in a working-class Scottish home, Slessor petitioned mission agencies for several year before she was appointed a teacher in Calabar, Nigeria, by Scotland's United Presbyterian Church. From the start, her superiors recognized her unusual zeal but also worried about her independent spirit. In 1888, she was dispatched to live among the Okoyong where she went barefoot, dressed in nearly native garb, and maintained a refuge for ostracized women and for the twins she rescued from abandonment. When Britain expanded its control over northern Nigeria, Slessor visited the furthest outposts where she established refuges for African women and children. She was one of the first modern missionaries to conceive of mission as the indigenization of Christianity rather than an importation from the West.

In the 20th century, more and more women exercised public roles at home like those missionary women had been filling abroad. The American Methodist deacon Georgia Harkness became a key participant in early meetings of Life and Work and the World Council of Churches, while her older contemporary, the Baptist scholar, Helen Barrett Montgomery, was a notable promoter of missions as well as an accomplished translator of Scripture. At the first general assembly of the World Council of Churches in 1948, Harkness defended the ordination of women in a spirited exchange with Karl Barth in which she gave as good as she got. The entire direction of church education in American evangelical churches was decisively shaped by Henrietta Mears, who besides running a successful publishing company and conference centre, taught hundreds of young people at First Presbyterian Church, Hollywood, California, aided Fuller Theological Seminary in its early years, and pushed a young Bill Bright toward the ministry that eventually became Campus Crusade for Christ International.

After mid-century, many traditional mainline denominations joined the Wesleyan, Holiness, and Pentecostal denominations that had long allowed women to serve as pastors. This departure from traditional practice worried, and continues to worry, some confessional and conservative Protestants. But by the end of the century broader public participation by women in church activities throughout much of the Protestant world had become an accepted fact of life. This change assured that questions of family, procreation, gender, domestic economy, and healthcare have received attention with broader resources of scriptural exegesis and life experience than was the case when men monopolized the churches' public life.

Ecumenical trajectories from the 19th century have also continued to expand. The 349 member organizations of the World Council of Churches (WCC) include many Protestant denominations, especially from the older European and American churches and from churches in the rest of the world connected to them. Much of the new energy in ecumenicity has come from the local fellowships formed by the evangelicals, fundamentalists, pentecostals, Anabaptists, conservative Lutherans, and holiness denominations that do not belong to the WCC. Just as effective, and often better financed, are NGOs like the Mennonite Central Committee and World Vision that mobilize increasing numbers of volunteers and employ large professional staff for effective development work motivated by Christian concern. The Lausanne Congress on World Evangelization of 1974, which was sponsored by the Billy Graham Evangelistic Association, drew 2,700 delegates from more countries and more denominations than any other international Protestant meeting ever held to that time.

The ministries growing out of the work of individual preachers and 'public Christians' also deliver significant ecumenical results. The worldwide travels of Billy Graham – as also similar journeys by the American faith-healer Oral Roberts, the Anglican Bible expositor John R. W. Stott, and the Pentecostal evangelist

Reinhard Bonnke – have functioned as powerful devices for creating broad networks of believers.

Ecumenism of a hitherto unthinkable sort also became much more important in the last decades of the 20th century. This activity involved Protestants in productive discussion with Romans Catholics, in effect restarting the discussions that had been broken off at the Council of Regensburg in 1541. The stalemate began to dissolve as a result of the Second Vatican Council (1962–5), which Pope John XXIII convened in order to breathe new life into his communion. The Council's treatment of non-Catholic Christians (as well as of non-Christian religions in general) was much gentler than that previously, and this visible softening led to a series of official dialogues initiated by the Vatican. In the decades after the Council, ecumenism among Protestants and between Protestants and Catholics has also increased in parts of the world where minority Christian churches confront majority Islam.

The high point to date of discussions sparked by Vatican II was the announcement by the Vatican and the Lutheran World Federation in October 1997 that a substantial measure of official agreement had been reached on the doctrine of justification by faith. This crux of the Protestant Reformation had historically been one of the great sticking points with the Catholic Church. Now, however, the joint committee declared that Catholics and Lutherans could agree on two essentials: God redeemed humans freely and only by his grace; redeemed humans properly responded to the reception of God's grace by doing good works.

De-Christianization in Europe

The greatest discontinuity in recent history is the manifest weakening of European Protestant churches since the middle of the 20th century. For many regions where one-quarter to one-half, or more, of the people regularly attended church, now steady participation has fallen well below one-tenth of Protestant populations. De-Christianization could come with a rush, as when the Nazis strong-armed German churches to exchange traditional Christianity for a semi-pagan Hitlerism. Much more typically it has occurred incrementally as material goods, therapy, politics, commerce, or entertainment edge aside historic church commitments.

A provocative thesis by the British sociologist, Collum Brown, has offered one broad explanation for the recent changes. In his reading, Christianity remained central to European society so long as it provided the most important vocabulary for defining existence and so long as it retained the loyalty of women, who had always transmitted Christianity to the rising generation. In Brown's account, the Christian frame of reference gave way in the 1950s. Prosperity, new forms of entertainment, the pervasive presence of television, and a new striving for personal fulfilment all reflected a new approach to life in general. When large numbers of women began to view themselves as autonomous actors in modern society, de-Christianization became even more pronounced.

Whatever the exact sequence of cause and effect, Brown and other observers were certainly right in noting seismic changes in European religious life after the 1950s. Church attendance declined sharply everywhere, with Scandinavia and other centres of centralized, official Protestantism showing the steepest drop-offs. Even the most casual references to God could generate noisy opposition, as when a proposal was made to mention Europe's Christian heritage in the Constitution of the European Union.

Yet de-Christianization is not the only post-war story. It is remarkable that the public demonstrations of 1989 that led to regime change in both East Germany and Romania began in churches where some residue of Protestant teaching remained alive. In Romania, the Communist dictatorship cracked when it was unable to silence a popular Reformed pastor, Lazlo Tokes, in the city of Timisoara. In East Germany in 1989, hundreds, then thousands, and finally tens of thousand, gathered peacefully for prayer meetings in Lutheran churches, including St Nicolai's in Leipzig where Bach had conducted his cantatas 250 years before. These meetings were instrumental in softening the regime and leading to the peaceful dismantling of the Berlin Wall in November 1989.

It is not difficult to find other signs of life. The Lutheran churches of Germany sponsor a biennial Kirchentag (church day) that draws together assemblages of 100,000 or more to pray, listen to sermons, and heighten connections with other believers worldwide. In parallel with Catholics, the German Lutheran churches also maintain an active and effective organization in Berlin that consults regularly on issues affecting moral and religious policy.

Europe's new immigrants also boost Protestant vitality. Many commentators have noted the religious changes in Europe from the growing numbers of Muslims. Fewer have remarked on how significant the new Christian immigration has become, including many churches serving African immigrants in France, large congregations filled with Caribbean and African newcomers in England, and Sunday Adelaja's Pentecostal church in Kiev.

An American exception?

In comparative perspective, it is striking that as American society throughout the 20th century has became affluent, modern, and diverse, it has not tracked what happened when Europe became more modern, affluent, and diverse. In measurable terms of regular church adherence, professed belief in God, financial support of religious institutions, and salience of religion in political debate, the United States has seemed to adjust better to modern circumstances.

Some have argued that Americans practise a thin form of Christianity, with the conventions of individualistic and consumer-driven culture dictating the content and form of religious life. Others note that American education, mass media, the courts, and government at all levels now heed guidance from the churches only on rare occasions. It has even been argued that the difference between secularism in the United States and Europe is that it takes place within the American churches instead of as a force driving people from the churches.

But even with legitimate questions about quality control, the situation remains clear: by comparison with Europe, there are more people in the United States who actively practise Protestant faiths, the vitality of Protestant churches and voluntary organizations is greater, and the influence of Protestants in public life is more visible.

The make-up of American Protestantism is, however, changing fast. Over the last half-century, the once dominant mainline churches (Methodist, Presbyterian, Lutheran, Episcopal, and Congregational), while maintaining large and relatively well-funded denominations, have yielded public space to a multitude of more evangelical, fundamentalist, Pentecostal, sectarian, holiness, independent, and immigrant churches. Careful empirical research suggests that mainline Protestants now make up about 15% of the American population, with another 26% in mostly Caucasian evangelical or conservative Protestant churches and 9% in the largely Protestant African American churches (the other half of the populace divides 20% Catholic, 10% other religious groups, and 20% functionally unattached).

One of the large developments that brought sharply focused Christian morality back into the American public square was the civil rights movement of the 1950s and 1960s. Its leading spokesman was the black Baptist minister, Martin Luther King, Jr, who skilfully combined pacifism from India's Mahatma Gandhi with much from traditional African American Christianity. King's most loyal supporters were ordinary church-goers from black Methodist and Baptist churches who practised basic biblical faith. Together, leaders and followers pushed the United States to extend civil rights to its African American communities that had long suffered systematic discrimination.

Continuity with a difference: politics

Much world attention has focused on the American Protestants who came after the black civil rights leaders and who also brought direct religious influence into politics. These have been largely conservative white evangelicals. Although most white evangelicals eventually accepted civil rights for black Americans, many objected to the expansion of government authority it took to enforce civil rights. Even more, they objected when court rulings and federal legislation banned prayer and Bible reading in the public schools, legalized abortion on demand, and relaxed restrictions against homosexual practice. The result was a 'New Christian Right'. This political movement linked conservative white Protestants to the Republican Party and played a significant role in electing presidents Ronald Reagan (1980 and 1984) and George W. Bush (2000 and 2004). The lessons for Protestants elsewhere in the world was to show how much political influence a well-organized religious cadre could exert in a modern democracy, but also how difficult it was to maintain the integrity of faith when religious and political goals intermingled in hot public contention.

Observers of the strong link between evangelical Protestants and right-wing politics in the United States have sometimes assumed that Protestant politics in the non-Western world is also uniformly right wing, since most Protestant or Protestant-like groups in these regions are evangelical, Pentecostal, independent, or sectarian in some fashion. The actual situation, however, is more complicated. Paul Freston, a student of Brazil's burgeoning Protestant networks, has concluded that recent research 'challenges facile equations of evangelicalism with conservative stances [and shows] the distance of these actors – indeed, total independence of these actors – from the American evangelical right'.

As with so many aspects of recent Protestant history, the most prominent feature of Protestant politics is diversity. There is Frederick Chiluba who shortly after his election as president of Zambia in 1991, proclaimed his country a 'Christian nation'. There is Brazil, where representatives of the Universal Church of the Kingdom of God, which was founded only in the 1970s, have served in parliament since the late 1980s (but there is also Chile, with about the same proportion of evangelical Protestants as Brazil, where no evangelicals have ever served in parliament). In South Africa, there was Nicholas Bhengu – founder of the 'Back to God' crusades, mobilizer of godly women, organizer of hundreds of churches – who mostly avoided politics yet helped undermine apartheid; Frank Chikane, a member of the Pentecostal Apostolic Faith Mission and forthright Christian layman who was such an active supporter of the African National Congress that he was asked to join the post-apartheid administration of Nelson Mandela; and also much Protestant support for the Truth and Reconciliation Commission.

The complexity of the world situation requires discriminating judgments. In some areas, political activism from new Protestant groups has been followed closely by corruption, favouritism, violent tribalism, and the other political maladies bedevilling the developing world. In particular, evangelicals and Pentecostals have been among the strongest supporters of oppressive regimes in Peru (under Alberto Fujimori), in Zambia when Chiluba became authoritarian, and in South Africa during the apartheid years. Parliamentary leaders of Brazil's Universal Church of the Kingdom of God have gone to prison for taking bribes, while Pentecostals, evangelicals, and members of African Independent churches have contributed to Kenya's simmering tribal strife from the time of Daniel arap Moi's regime to recent debates over laws concerning homosexuals and the public rights of Muslims. In the worst case, General Efraín Ríos Montt, the Sunday School teacher and Pentecostal elder who served as president of Guatemala from to 1982 to 1984 and has remained a political force, presided over some of the most systematic human-rights abuses and wanton violence in recent Latin American history.

But against these instances of Protestant complicity in political malfeasance are instances where Protestants have courageously supported human rights, the rule of law, and the growth of democracy. During the 1980s and 1990s, lay Pentecostals in Peru led the effort to form 'peasant patrols' that put their lives on the line to protect native communities against the Shining Path communist guerilla movement. Members of the Brazilian Parliament from the Universal Church of the Kingdom of God have manoeuvred with genuine political sophistication in working cooperatively with both right-leaning and left-leaning governments. In Zambia, evangelicals led the resistance to President Chiluba when he fell prey to the 'third termism' that has so often imperiled young African democracies. Most impressively, in Kenya a series of courageous Anglican bishops, led by David Gitari (Archbishop of the Anglican Church of Kenya, 1997–2002), has spoken truth to power on many occasions to chastise government corruption, defend basic human rights, and appeal for national harmony.

Worldwide

The truly stupendous changes in recent Protestant history have mostly taken place outside of the West. Simply to outline the big picture is to show the impossibility of taking it all in: by the mid-20th century, Protestant communities of considerable strength were flourishing in many parts of the world where there had been no, or virtually no, Protestant presence a century and a half before. These included, as a very partial list: Japan, Korea, China, the Dutch East Indies, Melanesia, Polynesia, Australia, and

New Zealand; Manipur, Nagaland, and many other parts of India; many countries in West Africa, East Africa, and South Africa, Madagascar and Mauritius; Greenland, Brazil, Guatemala, Chile, the Lesser Antilles, and Jamaica (not to speak of the United States west of the Appalachians or Canada west of Quebec).

In Latin America, careful polling in the early 21st century revealed that one-fifth or more of the residents in Belize, Brazil, Costa Rica, the Dominican Republic, El Salvador, Guatemala, Honduras, and Nicaragua told researchers they were Protestants of some sort. Agents of the British and Foreign Bible Society had been allowed to distribute Scriptures in a few Latin countries as early as the 1830s. Protestant missionaries were working in many parts of Latin America by 1900. And migrations of European Lutherans, Mennonites, and other traditional bodies had taken place before the mid-20th century. Representatives of these earlier Protestant groups thrive in scattered Latin American locations. But the surge in Protestant church expansion has come mostly over the last sixty years. It has been a feature of the region's rapid globalization. And it has been overwhelmingly Pentecostal in one form or another.

The sociologist and historian David Martin has interpreted the rapid rise of Protestant movements in Latin America and other rapidly globalizing societies as similar to the earlier spread of Methodism in rapidly industrializing Britain. In both cases, tumultuous social change means 'increasing speed of movement, as peoples, ideas, images, and capital take advantage of modern means of communication'. A take-off in urban population often accelerates powerful upsets of traditional society. People are shaken out of the given certainties of time-honoured relationships while experiencing a heightened sense of the self as both threatened and empowered by modernity. In these conditions, forms of the faith flourish that emphasize the power of God to speak directly to individuals, to provide discipline from within, and to create supportive communities of like-minded believers. As Martin has summarized a broad sweep of Christian history:

13. The Korean evangelist Billy Kim hands Fidel Castro, the communist leader of Cuba, a Spanish-language Bible

Once the Bible is your text there are as many interpretations as there are readers, and the Spirit is unbound. Traditionally that has been accounted one of the disadvantages of Evangelical Protestantism, since it replaces one Pope by a multitude, and dissipates energies in passionate dispute. In today's world, however, where the niches and needs are so varied, Pentecostalism works by constant adjustment on the ground.

Protestant expansion in Latin America is especially remarkable when it is remembered that at Edinburgh in 1910 the most savvy mission-minded Protestants in the world did not give Latin America a second glance.

One contemporary controversy illustrates how the Protestant world is changing because of what is happening in Africa. From the late

1920s, the five-country region of Uganda, Rwanda, Burundi, Kenya, and Tanzania was the scene of what came to be known as the East African Revival. Its character owed something to missionary propagation of Holiness themes from the English Keswick conference. Even more was owed to the ability of its main African preachers to make evangelical practices of confession, standards of morality, and doctrines of Christ's atonement come alive in African terms. The revival's *balokole*, or 'saved ones', sustained a tense relationship with their sponsors from the Anglican Church Missionary Society, but for the most part remained active in the Anglican communion. Well past the end of colonial rule, many associated with this revival practised a strongly pietist form of Christianity that concentrated on personal spiritual purity while disparaging active involvement in politics or social reform. From its origins, the movement steadily gained more adherents and gradually moved out beyond its original sphere of influence. Tragically, the spread of revival into Rwanda and Burundi did not do much to quell the tribal antagonism that climaxed in the great massacres of 1993.

But by its third generation, some leaders of the East African revival like Bishop Gitari in Kenya found themselves in positions of church leadership where they expanded their concerns from the strictly spiritual. In Uganda under Idi Amin, several distinguished products of the revival, like the Archbishop of Uganda Janani Luwum, were martyred for daring to resist the dictator's violent oppression. Such faithfulness unto death lent extraordinary credibility to the religion the martyrs espoused.

By the early 21st century, 40% of Uganda's more than 22 million people were counted as Anglicans, and with a far higher proportion actively involved in church life than had become the pattern for Anglicans and Episcopalians in the Western world. Large and growing Anglican communions were also found in the other Great Lakes nations. Over the same period, a different set of circumstances had led to substantial growth of Anglican populations in Nigeria and other West African countries.

When, therefore, the worldwide Anglican communion began its discussions of the decisions taken by the American Episcopal Church to ordain practising homosexuals as bishops and by some dioceses of the Anglican Church of Canada to bless same-sex marriages, the new shape of world Protestantism created a problem. The burgeoning Anglican churches of East Africa had been strongly influenced by a long-standing revival that insisted on sexual purity in heterosexual marriage. They had been criticized by African Independent Churches for bending to missionary dictates when they put an end to practices that the indigenous churches continued (in particular, polygamy and female genital mutilation). And with Africans of all kinds far beyond the Anglican, or even Christian, churches, they had recently mobilized to fight the scourge of HIV/AIDS.

African Anglican bishops who took the lead in criticizing their Western sister churches had come of age in the postcolonial era. They were, therefore, not cowed when a few members of the Western churches responded to their criticisms with threats of withholding funds or other forms of Western aid. The jargon of subaltern postcolonialism may have sounded unusual in concert with strongly conservative appeals to Scripture, but it was a natural combination for the Africans who stood firmly for their interpretation of the gospel.

If possible, the recent history in China is even more remarkable. During Mao Zedong's Great Proletarian Cultural Revolution of 1966 to 1976, every church, Catholic and Protestant, was shuttered throughout this vast nation. In the decades since, the resurgence of Christianity has been astounding, and that resurgence has owed very little to direct Western influence. The ground that Chinese Catholics have regained, despite intense

14. A woman at prayer in contemporary China

jurisdictional disputes, would be the greatest story of advance in modern Christian history were it not for the even more rapid expansion of Protestant groups. Many of the most rapidly advancing Protestant bodies are direct or indirect descendents of Chinese movements that had already become at least quasi-independent before missionaries were expelled when Mao came to power in 1949. So long as the missionaries were present, the Chinese churches linked most closely to the West loomed largest in public view. Even after that departure, Westerners were most familiar with churches of the Three-Self Patriotic Movement that allowed themselves to be registered under the communist government.

Yet already by mid-century, there were several important streams of Chinese Protestants who, if they had arisen through missionary contact, had already begun to make their own way. These included the pentecostal True Jesus Church (founded 1917), the strongly communal Jesus Family (1921), and the Little Flock or Local Church directed from the mid-1920s by Watchman Nee (Ni Tuosheng) who had been converted under Dora Yu. In addition, many converts from the passionate ministry in the 1930s of John Sung (Song Shangjie) and his Bethel Band turned out to have as much staying power as the Kimbanguists of central Africa. The quasi-fundamentalist but fiercely independent Wang Mingdao had also achieved a significant following in and around Beijing.

These and similar indigenous Chinese movements have driven the recent surge of Christian adherence among rural and urban Chinese. Curiosity about Christianity from China's best-educated elites may have much to do with interest in how classical Christianity might regulate the rush to economic individualism. With the presence of flourishing churches in cities and the countryside alike, the future development of Christianity should be one of the most telling stories of the 21st century.

Commonalities

With the great diversity of worldwide Protestantism, an unexpectedly large number of commonalities still remain. Europeans and some Americans still think in terms of carefully defined organizations to express such commonalities, but loose networks gathered for specific projects or individual initiatives are now responsible for more of what Germans call *Mitgefühl* (a sense of belonging together). Scripture, about which Protestants argue among themselves incessantly, remains the key point of contact. If the arguments would ever stop, then Protestantism would no longer have any central meaning at all.

But there are many others, like the continuing Western leadership in theological education. Protestant colleges, universities, and seminaries have for some time been popping up at a breakneck pace – in Kenya, India, Nigeria, Korea, Central and South America, and elsewhere. Yet Protestants from all over the globe still look to the West for advanced educational guidance.

Another increasingly common feature of Protestants worldwide is the music. But here there are two quite different forces at work, one indigenous and the other globalizing. In many individual places, newly translated Scriptures and other Christian material is being set to local traditional music with dramatically effective results. These musics usually sound completely distinct; the common feature is the principle of translation applied to music.

Globalizing Protestant music reflects the ubiquity of the Internet. It is often marked by exuberance, spontaneity, subjective lyrics, and the exploitation of pop, folk, and soft rock style. Although these impulses owe much to charismatic influence, even churches that have not embraced Pentecostal or charismatic principles now often reflect in public worship a line of influence that began at Azusa Street.

Throughout the world, almost all Protestant groups now pay more attention to the power and work of the Holy Spirit, some by practising the sign-gifts like speaking in tongues and divine healing, others by renewed attention to prayer, fasting, and other spiritual disciplines.

And the list could go on. But since one of the primary features of what world Protestantism has become is the open-ended character of even its commonalities, it is time to stop.

Conclusion

For several centuries, Protestants treated Catholics as opposing everything for which they stood (and the sentiment was reciprocated). But for both groups the broad assumptions of Christendom prevailed. Most Protestants long practised their religion by assuming it was part of a traditional Christian civilization with well-defined parameters of Christian belief, church–state cooperation, and cohesive social expectations. When European Christianity came to the American colonies and evolved in the development of the United States, a second type of Protestantism arose. By stressing voluntary organization, it represented the successful adaptation of traditional European Christendom to a liberal social environment. Over the course of the 19th century, voluntary and unregulated churches made the United States the most dynamic centre of Protestant expansion the world had yet seen.

From the early 20th century, and with the rapid spread of Christianity outside the West, yet a third type of Protestantism has arisen. While often connected to Europe or America, especially through missionaries, this third type reflects the religious effects of globalization. Protestant churches outside Europe and North America usually practise the free-form voluntarism of American churches, but often in competition with many new forces – with Islam or Hinduism or primal religions, with grinding poverty and massive urbanization, and with Asian or African economic and political realities.

Protestantism is, thus, presently constituted by three distinct expressions of the Christian religion – proprietary (with European origins), voluntary (with America as the exemplar), and global (keyed to recent world conditions). As if these forms did not create enough diversity, Protestantism is also overlaid with a multitude of doctrinal differences, differing musical forms, different political attitudes, and huge differences in wealth and kinds of social power.

The result is a religion that, though sharing many specific teachings and moral principles with Catholicism, is closer in form to Judaism or Islam. Shared reference to a sacred text provides a point of convergence, but multiple traditions for interpreting that text, multiple authorities proclaiming the text, and multiple contexts in which the text is appropriated create a loose field of experiences and truth claims rather than anything coherent.

To ask what Martin Luther would or would not recognize in, say, the proliferating Protestant or Protestant-like movements in Africa today is to make the problem of Protestant cohesion concrete. Luther might be amazed and gratified by the rapid recent growth of Africa's Lutheran churches that share his appeal to the authority of Scripture.

He might be mystified by Josiah M. Kibira of Tanzania, the first African president of the Lutheran World Federation (1977–84), who cooperates with the leaders of the Anglican-led East African Revival who brought him to faith. About a trip to Germany that Kabira once took, Luther would have recognized the sentiment: Kabira reported that a few German Lutherans told him that he could not really be a Lutheran inasmuch as he abstained from alcohol!

Lutherans in Africa

Lutheran churches in Ethiopia, Tanzania, and Malagasy now have as many members as the largest Lutheran denominations in the United States.

1970	1995	2008
Ethiopian Evangelical Church Mekane Yesus		
177,000	2,000,000	4,500,000
Evangelical Lutheran Church in Tanzania		
592,000	2,200,000	3,500,000
Eglise Lutherienne Malgacha (Malagasy)		
448,200	852,000	3,000,000

On more substantial matters, Luther would be thoroughly discomfited by Africa's Protestant pluralism, which has failed spectacularly in achieving the reformed and unified Christendom he sought. More distressing would be the theological pluralism, with many doctrines now popular in Africa drawn from a huge array of biblical approaches, only a few of which come close to his own biblical convictions.

Yet if Luther could talk with contemporary African Lutherans who are with him deeply committed to 'justification by grace through faith', it might be a different story. When Joseph Ngah participated in a meeting of the Lutheran World Federation in 2000, he addressed justification directly. Luther would have been pleased to hear Ngah affirm that justification means salvation 'not only from the demands of God's law but also from the powers that keep [sinners] in bondage. These powers are death, sin, the devil, and the wrath of God.' Ngah actually came closer to Luther's own views than many Western Lutherans when he detailed

15. A church service in the Utondolo Lutheran Cathedral, Lushoto, Tanzania

supernatural foes of the sort that Luther also battled: 'Satanism, magical practices, witchcraft, and secret societies'. But Luther would have to pause to take in what Ngah said next: modern Africans are plagued with 'numerous other tyrants' like 'economic subjugation', dependence on foreign countries, hunger, poverty, and social-economic and sociopolitical evils 'peculiar to Africans' that also need the remedy of justifying grace.

For Luther, the distance that such a modern Protestantism had travelled from his own day would not be the whole story. Almost certainly he would rejoice in the hundreds of fresh translations that over the course of the last century have made the Bible accessible to more and more Africans in their native languages. He might also appreciate evidence concerning the ongoing importance of 'the priesthood of all believers' that lay behind the advertisements recently observed in Ghana for businesses called 'Jesus Is King Metal Works' and 'Christ Is God Plumbing Works'.

It is even possible that, despite the Protestant diversity created by the sweep of world events and internal Protestant disposition to going it alone, Luther might even be able to detect commonality in things that he cared about most. The painters who worked under the patronage of early Lutheran rulers sometimes put the leading figures of their day into the biblical scenes they drew. One of the most famous of such examples is the Weimar Altarpiece painted by Lucas Cranach the Elder and his son. It depicts Luther standing with an open Bible beside the cross of Christ; from the crucified side of Christ jets a crimson stream that symbolizes the blood of Christ shed for human sin.

This imagery is pure 16th-century German, but a modern artist might be able to paint something similar about one of the most compelling individuals documented in Diane Stinton's path-breaking book, *Jesus of Africa*. Nana Dokua, queen mother of the Akuapem traditional area of southern Ghana, was seventy-six years old when Stinton interviewed her in the late 1990s. This illiterate matriarch recounted how she had once been so sick she could not walk, but that then she had felt the touch of Jesus: 'He's my healer, my doctor. Formerly, I couldn't walk properly. Now I can run! *Yes!*' Most telling was what Nana Dokua said about her experience of childlessness in a society that places supreme value on motherhood. If Martin Luther could listen, he would hear echoes of what he had written in paraphrasing Psalm 46 as the defining hymn of the Reformation: 'A mighty fortress is our God, a bulwark never failing.' When Nana Dokua told how she identified with the crucified Saviour for enabling her to transcend this grief, she spoke joyfully of Jesus' impact 'in everything! In all my ways. Jesus has been a good friend. A doctor, a healer! My protector! My fortress! My shield! Everything.'

Further reading

Reference works

David Barrett et al. (eds.), *World Christian Encyclopedia*, 2 vols (New York: Oxford University Press, 2001).

Harland P. Beach and Charles H. Fahs (eds.) *World Missionary Atlas* (New York: Institute of Social and Religious Research, 1925).

Biographical Dictionary of Chinese Christianity (online).

Dictionary of African Christian Biography (online).

Erwin Fahlbusch et al. (eds.), *The Encyclopedia of Christianity*, 5 vols (Grand Rapids: Eerdmans, 1999–2008).

Hans Hillerbrand (ed.), *The Encyclopedia of Protestantism*, 4 vols (New York: Routledge, 2004).

Todd M. Johnson and Kenneth R. Ross (eds.), *Atlas of World Christianity* (Edinburgh: Edinburgh University Press, 2010).

Alister E. McGrath and Darren E. Marks (eds.), *The Blackwell Encyclopedia of Protestantism* (Oxford: Blackwell, 2004).

Jason Mandryk, *Operation World 2010* (Colorado Springs: Biblica, 2010).

Jaroslav Pelikan and Valerie Hotchkiss (eds.), *Creeds and Confessions of Faith in the Christian Tradition*, 4 vols (New Haven: Yale University Press, 2003).

General studies

Sydney E. Ahlstrom, updated by David D. Hall, *A Religious History of the American People* (New Haven: Yale University Press, 2004).

David W. Bebbington, *Evangelicalism in Modern Britain: A History from the 1730s to the 1980s* (London: Unwin Hyman, 1989).

Sébastien Fath, *Les Protestants* (Paris: Le Cavalier Bleu, 2003).

Felipe Fernández-Armesto and Derek Wilson, *Reformations: A Radical Interpretation of Christianity and the World, 1500–2000* (New York: Scribner, 1996).

Ogbu Kalu (ed.), *African Christianity: An African Story* (Trenton, NJ: Africa World Press, 2007).

Wolfgang Lück, *Lebensform Protestantismus: Reformatisches Erbe in der Gegenwart* (Stuttgart: W. Kohlhammer, 1992).

Alister E. McGrath, *Christianity's Dangerous Idea: The Protestant Revolution* (New York: HarperOne, 2007).

Hugh McLeod, *Religion and the People of Western Europe, 1789–1989*, 2nd edn. (New York: Oxford University Press, 1997).

Martin E. Marty, *Protestantism* (New York: Holt, Rinehart and Winston, 1972).

Martin E. Marty, *Righteous Empire: The Protestant Experience in America* (New York: Dial, 1970).

Samuel Hugh Moffett, *A History of Christianity in Asia, vol. II: 1500–1900* (Maryknoll, NY: Orbis, 2005).

Mark A. Noll, *A History of Christianity in the United States and Canada* (Grand Rapids: Eerdmans, 1992).

Mark A. Noll, *Turning Points: Decisive Moments in the History of Christianity*, 2nd edn. (Grand Rapids: Baker, 2001).

Wilhelm Pauck, *The Heritage of the Reformation*, 2nd edn. (New York: Oxford University Press, 1968).

Dana L. Robert, *Christian Mission: How Christianity Became a World Religion* (Malden, MA: Wiley-Blackwell, 2009).

Paul Tillich, *The Protestant Era* (Chicago: University of Chicago Press, 1948).

Andrew Walls, *The Cross-Cultural Process in Christian History* (Maryknoll, NY: Orbis, 2002).

Andrew Walls, *The Missionary Movement in Christian History* (Maryknoll, NY: Orbis, 1996).

John Witte, Jr, and Frank S. Alexander (eds.), *The Teachings of Modern Protestantism on Law, Politics, and Human Nature* (New York: Columbia University Press, 2007).

Introduction

J. Kwabena Asamoah-Gyadu, 'African Initiated Christianity in Eastern Europe: Church of the "Embassy of God" in Ukraine', *International Bulletin of Missionary Research*, 30 (April 2006): 73–5.

Website: english.fgtv/yfgc.pdf (Yoido Full Gospel Church).
Website: hirr.hartsem.edu/megachurch/megachurches.html
(megachurches).

Chapter 1

Roland H. Bainton, *Here I Stand: A Life of Martin Luther* (New York: Abingdon-Cokesbury, 1950).

A. G. Dickens and John Tonkin, *The Reformation in Historical Thought* (Cambridge: Harvard University Press, 1985).

Bruce Gordon, *Calvin* (New Haven: Yale University Press, 2009).

Scott H. Hendrix, *Martin Luther: A Very Short Introduction* (New York: Oxford University Press, 2010).

R. Po-Chi Hsia (ed.), *A Companion to the Reformation World* (Oxford: Blackwell, 2004).

Robert Kolb, *Martin Luther: Confessor of the Faith* (New York: Oxford University Press, 2009).

Carter Lindberg, *The European Reformations* (Oxford: Blackwell, 1996).

Timothy F. Lull (ed.), *Martin Luther's Basic Theological Writings* (Minneapolis: Fortress, 1989).

Diarmaid MacCulloch, *The Reformation: A History* (New York: Viking, 2003).

Mark A. Noll (ed.), *Confessions and Catechisms of the Reformation* (Vancouver: Regent College Publishing, 2004).

Heiko A. Oberman, *Martin Luther: Man Between God and the Devil* (New Haven: Yale University Press, 1989).

Philip S. Watson, *Let God Be God! An Interpretation of the Theology of Martin Luther*, 2nd edn. (Philadelphia: Fortress, 1970).

George H. Williams, *The Radical Reformation*, 3rd edn. (Kirksville, MO: Truman State University Press, 2000).

Chapter 2

Philip Benedict, *Christ's Churches Purely Reformed: A Social History of Calvinism* (New Haven: Yale University Press, 2002).

John Butt (ed.), *The Cambridge Companion to Bach* (Cambridge: Cambridge University Press, 1997).

Patrick Collinson, *The Religion of Protestants: The Church in English Society, 1559–1625* (Oxford: Clarendon Press, 1982).

Ian Green, *Print and Protestantism in Early Modern England* (Oxford: Oxford University Press, 2000).

Peter Harrison, *The Bible, Protestantism, and the Rise of Modern Science* (Cambridge: Cambridge University Press, 1998).

Barbara Kiefer Lewalski, *Protestant Poetics and the Seventeenth-Century Religious Lyric* (Cambridge: Harvard University Press, 1979).

Hugh McLeod, *The Religious Crisis of the 1960s* (Oxford: Oxford University Press, 2007) – on 'Christendom'.

Richard A. Muller, *After Calvin: Studies in the Development of a Theological Tradition* (New York: Oxford University Press, 2003).

Margo Todd, *The Culture of Protestantism in Early Modern Scotland* (New Haven: Yale University Press, 2002).

E. John Walford, *Jacob van Ruisdael and the Perception of Landscape* (New Haven: Yale University Press, 1991).

Peter H. Wilson, *The Thirty Years War: Europe's Tragedy* (Cambridge: Harvard University Press, 2009).

Chapter 3

Christopher Boyd Brown, *Singing the Gospel: Lutheran Hymns and the Success of the Reformation* (Cambridge, MA: Harvard University Press, 2005).

Peter Erb (ed.), *Pietists: Selected Writings* (New York: Paulist, 1983).

David Hempton, *Methodism: Empire of the Spirit* (New Haven: Yale University Press, 2005).

D. Bruce Hindmarsh, *The Evangelical Conversion Narrative: Spiritual Autobiography in Early Modern England* (Oxford: Oxford University Press, 2005).

Thomas S. Kidd, *The Great Awakening: The Roots of Evangelical Christianity in Colonial America* (New Haven: Yale University Press, 2007).

George M. Marsden, *Jonathan Edwards: A Life* (New Haven: Yale University Press, 2003).

Mark A. Noll, *The Rise of Evangelicalism: The Age of Edwards, Whitefield, and the Wesleys* (Downers Grove, IL: InterVarsity Press, 2003).

Henry D. Rack, *Reasonable Enthusiast: John Wesley and the Rise of Methodism*, 3rd edn. (London: Epworth, 2002).

Harry S. Stout, *The Divine Dramatist: George Whitefield and the Rise of Modern Evangelicalism* (Grand Rapids: Eerdmans, 1991).

Mark R. Valeri, *Heavenly Merchandize: How Religion Shaped Commerce in Puritan America* (Princeton: Princeton University Press, 2010).

Patricia A. Ward, *Experimental Theology in America: Madame Guyon, Fénelon, and their Readers* (Waco, TX: Baylor University Press, 2009).

W. R. Ward, *Christianity under the Ancien Régime, 1648–1789* (Cambridge: Cambridge University Press, 1999).

W. R. Ward, *The Protestant Evangelical Awakening* (Cambridge: Cambridge University Press, 1992).

Chapter 4

David W. Bebbington, *The Dominance of Evangelicalism: The Age of Spurgeon and Moody* (Downers Grove, IL: InterVarsity Press, 2005).

James D. Bratt (ed.), *Abraham Kuyper: A Centennial Reader* (Grand Rapids: Eerdmans, 1998).

Richard Carwardine, *Transatlantic Revivalism: Popular Evangelicalism in Britain and America, 1790–1865* (Westport, CT: Greenwood, 1978).

Owen Chadwick, *The Secularization of the European Mind in the Nineteenth Century* (Cambridge: Cambridge University Press, 1975).

Walter H. Conser, *Church and Confession: Conservative Theologians in Germany, England, and America, 1815–1866* (Macon, GA: Mercer University Press, 1984).

Alexis de Tocqueville, *Democracy in America*, tr. Arthur Goldhammer (New York: Library of America, 2004).

Nathan O. Hatch, *The Democratization of American Christianity* (New Haven: Yale University Press, 1989).

Nicholas Hope, *German and Scandinavian Protestantism, 1700–1918*, Oxford History of Christianity (New York: Oxford University Press, 1995).

Hugh McLeod, *Secularization in Western Europe, 1848–1914* (New York: St Martin's, 2000).

Mark A. Noll, *The Civil War as a Theological Crisis* (Chapel Hill, NC: University of North Carolina Press, 2006).

Anne Stott, *Hannah More: The First Victorian* (New York: Oxford University Press, 2003).

Claude Welch, *Protestant Thought in the Nineteenth Century*, 2 vols (New Haven: Yale University Press, 1972, 1985).

John Wigger, *American Saint: Francis Asbury and the Methodists* (Oxford: Oxford University Press, 2009).

John Wolffe, *The Expansion of Evangelicalism: The Age of Wilberforce, More, Chalmers, and Finney* (Downers Grove, IL: InterVarsity Press, 2007).

Chapter 5

Alvyn Austin, *China's Millions: The China Inland Mission and Late Qing Society, 1832–1905* (Grand Rapids: Eerdmans, 2007).

Ian Breward, *A History of the Churches in Australia*, Oxford History of the Christian Church (New York: Oxford University Press, 2001).

Jeffrey Cox, *Imperial Faultlines: Christianity and Colonial Power in India, 1818–1940* (Stanford: Stanford University Press, 2002).

Katherine Carté Engle, *Religion and Profit: Moravians in Early America* (Philadelphia: University of Pennsylvania Press, 2009).

Robert Eric Frykenberg, *Christianity in India: From Beginnings to the Present*, Oxford History of the Christian Church (New York: Oxford University Press, 2008).

Daniel Jeyaraj, *Bartholomäus Ziegenbalg: The Father of the Modern Protestant Mission* (Delhi, India: ISPCK, 2007).

Stephen Neill, *A History of Christian Missions* (New York: Penguin, 1986).

John F. Sensbach, *Rebecca's Revival: Creating Black Christianity in the Atlantic World* (Cambridge, MA: Harvard University Press, 2005).

Brian Stanley, *The Bible and the Flag: Protestant Missions and British Imperialism in the Nineteenth and Twentieth Centuries* (Leicester, Eng.: Apollo, 1990).

Rachel M. Wheeler, *To Live Upon Hope: Mohicans and Missionaries in the Eighteenth-Century Northeast* (Ithaca: Cornell University Press, 2008).

Chapter 6

Allan Anderson, *An Introduction to Pentecostalism: Global Charismatic Christianity* (New York: Cambridge University Press, 2004).

David B. Barrett, *Schism and Renewal in Africa: An Analysis of Six Thousand Contemporary Religious Movements* (Nairobi: Oxford University Press, 1968).

Daniel Bays (ed.), *Christianity in China: From the Eighteenth Century to the Present* (Stanford: Stanford University Press, 1996).

Heather D. Curtis, *Faith in the Great Physician: Suffering and Divine Healing in American Culture, 1860–1900* (Baltimore: Johns Hopkins University Press, 2007).

Martinus Daneel, *Zionism and Faith-Healing in Rhodesia: Aspects of African Independent Churches* (Holland: Mouton, 1970).

Ogbu Kalu, *African Pentecostalism: An Introduction* (New York: Oxford University Press, 2008).

William K. Kay, *Pentecostalism: A Very Short Introduction* (New York: Oxford University Press, 2011).

David Martin, *Pentecostalism: The World Their Parish* (Oxford: Blackwell, 2002).

Pandita Ramabai through her own words, Selected Works (New Delhi: Oxford University Press, 2000).

David A. Shank, *Prophet Harris: The 'Black Elijah' of West Africa* (Leiden: Brill, 1994).

W. T. Stead. *The Story of the Welsh Revival* (New York: Fleming H. Revell, 1905).

Grant Wacker, *Heaven Below: Early Pentecostals and American Culture* (Cambridge, MA: Harvard University Press, 2001).

Chapter 7

Joel A. Carpenter, *Revive Us Again: The Reawakening of American Fundamentalism* (New York: Oxford University Press, 1997).

John Webster Grant, *The Church in the Canadian Era*, 2nd edn. (Burlington, Ontario: Welch, 1988).

Susan Billington Harper, *In the Shadow of the Mahatma: Bishop V. S. Azariah and the Travails of Christianity in India* (Grand Rapids: Eerdmans, 2000).

George M. Marsden, *Fundamentalism and American Culture*, 2nd edn. (New York: Oxford University Press, 2006).

Martin E. Marty, *Modern American Religion*, 3 vols (Chicago: University of Chicago Press, 1986–96).

Dana Robert, *American Women in Mission* (Macon, GA: Mercer University Press, 1996).

Brian Stanley, *The World Missionary Conference: Edinburgh 1910* (Grand Rapids: Eerdmans, 2009).

John Webster (ed.), *The Cambridge Companion to Karl Barth* (Cambridge: Cambridge University Press, 2000).

Chapter 8

Callum Brown, *The Death of Christian Britain: Christianity and Secularization, 1800–2000* (New York: Routledge, 2001).

Callum Brown and Michael Snape (eds.), *Secularisation in the Christian World, Essays in Honour of Hugh McLeod* (Farnham, Surrey: Ashgate, 2010).

Joel Carpenter and Wilbert R. Shenk (eds.), *Earthen Vessels: American Evangelicals and Foreign Missions, 1880–1980* (Grand Rapids: Eerdmans, 1990).

Mark Chaves, *Ordaining Women: Culture and Conflict in Religious Organizations* (Cambridge, MA: Harvard University Press, 1997).

Grace Davie, *Religion in Britain since 1945: Believing Without Belonging* (Oxford: Blackwell, 1994).

Paul Freston, *Evangelicals and Politics in Asia, Africa, and Latin America* (New York: Cambridge University Press, 2001).

Paul Freston (ed.), *Evangelical Christianity and Democracy in Latin America* (New York: Oxford University Press, 2008).

Jehu Hanciles, *Beyond Christendom: Globalization, African Migration, and the Transformation of the West* (Maryknoll, NY: Orbis, 2008).

Philip Jenkins, *The Next Christendom: The Coming of Global Christianity* (New York: Oxford University Press, 2002).

Philip Jenkins, *The New Faces of Christianity: Believing in the Bible in the Global South* (New York: Oxford University Press, 2006).

Xi Lian, *Redeemed by Fire: The Rise of Popular Christianity in China* (New Haven: Yale University Press, 2010).

David Lumsdane (ed.), *Evangelical Christianity and Democracy in Asia* (New York: Oxford University Press, 2009).

David Martin, *Tongues of Fire: The Explosion of Protestantism in Latin America* (Oxford: Blackwell, 1990).

Anthony O. Nkwoka, 'The Role of the Bible in the Igbo Christianity of Nigeria', in *The Bible in Africa: Transactions, Trajectories and Trends* (Boston: Brill Academic, 2001), pp. 326–35.

Mark A. Noll, *The New Shape of World Christianity: How American Experience Reflects Global Faith* (Downers Grove, IL: InterVarsity Press, 2009).

T. O. Ranger (ed.), *Evangelical Christianity and Democracy in Africa* (New York: Oxford University Press, 2008).

Lamin Sanneh, *Translating the Message* (Maryknoll, NY: Orbis, 1989).

Protestantism

Conclusion

Josiah Kabira, 'Has Luther Reached Africa: The Testimony of a
Confused Lutheran', *Africa Theological Journal*, 12:1 (1983): 6–15.

Joseph Ngah, 'Liberation from Evil Powers – Africa', in *Justification
in the World's Context*, LWF Documentation no. 45, ed. Wolfgang
Greive (Geneva: Lutheran World Federation, 2000), pp. 133–8.

Diane Stinton, *Jesus of Africa: Voices of Contemporary African
Christology* (Maryknoll, NY: Orbis, 2004).

Further reading

Glossary

adherents: since counting Protestants has always been an inexact science, a general term like 'adherents' is necessary in order to include those in churches where membership comes via an initiation rite (like baptism), those where membership is by a self-selecting action, and those where regular participation takes place without formal membership.

canon (Protestant): the Protestant canon of Scripture includes 39 Old Testament and 27 New Testament books. It does not include the deuterocanonical books that are part of Catholic Bibles.

charismatic: see page 91.

Christendom: see the definition from Hugh McLeod, page 29.

confession: confessions are statements of faith that were frequently used to identify territories by religious tradition during the era of Protestant Christendom.

denomination: this term, from the Latin for 'named', designates subgroups within Protestantism.

dissent: dissent means simply protest, but it was used in a technical sense for English Protestants who objected to the established Church of England.

ecumenism/ecumenical: ecumenism speaks of efforts by churches to cooperate or come together in unity; the World Council of Churches and the Lausanne Congress on World Evangelization are prominent contemporary examples.

evangelical: evangelical Protestants stress the Bible as final authority, the cross of Christ as their key theological principle, the need for conversion (or a 'new birth'), and the importance of actively following Christ.

evangelization (versus proselytization): evangelization is the process of spreading the good news (or 'gospel') of God's love revealed in Jesus Christ; proselytization has a negative connotation that implies manipulation or coercion in spreading Christianity.

fundamentalism: the word arose in the United States among revivalistic Protestants who wanted to preserve the fundamentals, or basics, of Christian faith. It has come to be used of traditionalist or anti-modern religious groups of all sorts.

gospel: the gospel is the 'good news' that Jesus Christ as the full revelation of God offers forgiveness of sin and participation in the building of God's kingdom.

health and wealth: some neo-Pentecostals and other contemporary Protestants preach that God desires all of his children to live healthy, prosperous lives, which believers should seek as an accepted goal of their faith.

Holy Spirit: the third member of the Christian Trinity whose work of building God's Kingdom is particularly stressed by modern Pentecostal churches.

independent: churches that acknowledge no connection to previously existing ecclesiastical bodies are called independent.

liberal: in social and political terms, liberal means societies oriented to individualism and free-market economics; in religious terms, liberal means a willingness to modify traditional Christian faith in accordance with contemporary intellectual or social conventions.

mainline: in recent history, mainline refers to older Protestant churches that were once pre-eminent in American and Canadian societies.

Nonconformists: Nonconformists are English Protestants who do not conform to the beliefs or practices of the established Church of England.

Pentecostal: see page 91.

Protestant-like: careful students of modern Christianity categorize many modern movements and groups, especially in the non-Western world, as 'independents' because they often acknowledge little or no connection with historic Protestant denominations. Many of them, however, closely resemble historical Protestant movements with their stress on the Bible, personal salvation, and the activity of local believers.

Puritans: ardent Protestants in England and the American colonies who in the 16th and 17th centuries wanted to carry the Reformation to what they considered its logical conclusions were known as Puritans.

revival/revivalist: revival is the renewal of active Christian faith in communities where it has grown stale. Revivalists are preachers or organizers who work to that end.

sects/sectarian: sectarian churches look mostly to the integrity of their own religious lives without devoting significant time or energy to influencing broader society. 'Proprietary' is an antonym for 'sectarian'.

Trinity: the Trinity is the classical Christian understanding that the one, unified God exists in three 'persons' (Father, Son, and Holy Spirit).

Index

Z

Zambia 126
Zedong, Mao 130, 132
Zeisberger, David 77

Ziegenbalg, Bartholomäus
74–5
Zinzendorf, Ludwig Nicholas
von 46, 77
Zwingli, Ulrich 19–22

Expand your collection of
VERY SHORT INTRODUCTIONS

CHRISTIANITY
A Very Short Introduction
Linda Woodhead

At a time when Christianity is flourishing in the Southern hemisphere but declining in much of the West, this *Very Short Introduction* offers an important new overview of the world's largest religion.

Exploring the cultural and institutional dimensions of Christianity, and tracing its course over two millennia, this book provides a fresh, lively, and candid portrait of its past and present. Addressing topics that other studies neglect, including the competition for power between different forms of Christianity, the churches' uses of power, and their struggles with modernity, Linda Woodhead concludes by showing the ways in which those who previously had the least power in Christianity— women and non-Europeans—have become increasingly central to its unfolding story.

'her analysis is subtle and perceptive.'
Independent on Sunday

www.oup.com/vsi/

ISLAM
A Very Short Introduction
Malise Ruthven

Islam features widely in the news, often in its most
militant versions, but few people in the non-Muslim
world really understand the nature of Islam.

Malise Ruthven's Very Short Introduction contains
essential insights into issues such as why Islam has such
major divisions between movements such as the Shi'ites,
the Sunnis, and the Wahhabis, and the central importance
of the Shar'ia (Islamic law) in Islamic life. It also
offers fresh perspectives on contemporary questions:
Why is the greatest 'Jihad' (holy war) now against the
enemies of Islam, rather than the struggle against evil?
Can women find fulfilment in Islamic societies? How
must Islam adapt as it confronts the modern world?

'Malise Ruthven's book answers the urgent need for an
introduction to Islam. ... He addresses major issues with
clarity and directness, engages dispassionately with the
disparate stereotypes and polemics on the subject, and
guides the reader surely through urgent debates about
fundamentalism.'

Michael Gilsenan, New York University

PENTECOSTALISM
A Very Short Introduction
William K. Kay

In religious terms Pentecostalism was probably the most
vibrant and rapidly-growing religious movement of the 20th
century. Starting as a revivalistic and renewal movement within
Christianity, it encircled the globe in less than 25 years and
grew in North America and then in those parts of the world
with the highest birth-rates. Characterised by speaking in
tongues, miracles, television evangelism and megachurches, it
is also noted for its small-group meetings, empowerment of
individuals, liberation of women and humanitarian concerns.
William K Kay outlines the origins and growth of
Pentecostalism, looking at not only the theological aspects of
the movement, but also the sociological influences of its
political and humanitarian viewpoints.

www.oup.com/vsi